INTERNET HOLD'EM POKER

Plus 5- and 7-card stud and Omaha

To My Wonderful Aunt Elaine

◇◇◇◇◇◇◇◇◇◇◇◇◇◇◇◇◇◇◇◇◇◇◇◇◇◇◇◇◇◇◇◇◇◇◇◇◇◇

Acknowledgments

Thanks to James Stern and Mans Ullerstam from cardozagames.com for fact-checking and technical information, Sam Ladlow for cover design and screenshots, and G. Blondini for a wonderful layout.

◇◇◇◇◇◇◇◇◇◇◇◇◇◇◇◇◇◇◇◇◇◇◇◇◇◇◇◇◇◇◇◇◇◇◇◇◇◇

About the Author

Avery Cardoza is the world's foremost authority on gambling, a multimillion-selling author of 21 books, and the publisher of the acclaimed national lifestyle magazine, *Avery Cardoza's Player*. His poker books include *How to Play Winning Poker*, *Poker Talk*, *The Basics of Winning Poker*, *The Basics of Winning Hold'em Poker* and *Crash Course in Beating Texas Hold'em Poker*.

Cardoza is a frequent money-winner and regular player in the high stakes poker championships seen on television. He has crippled the stacks of, or eliminated, more than a dozen world champions from major tournament competitions.

In 2007, leveraging more than 25 years as the oldest and most established gaming brand for players, Cardoza launched cardozagames.com, an online poker-playing site dealing honest games to players around the world.

Visit www.cardozapub.com for a full list of Cardoza Publishing books and www.cardozagames.com to learn more about playing poker online with the "Player's Brand."

INTERNET HOLD'EM POKER

Plus 5- and 7-card stud and Omaha

AVERY CARDOZA

CARDOZA PUBLISHING

Cardoza Publishing is the foremost gaming publisher in the world, with a library of over 200 up-to-date and easy-to-read books and strategies. These authoritative works are written by the top experts in their fields and with more than 10,000,000 books in print, represent the best-selling and most popular gaming books anywhere.

FIRST EDITION

Library of Congress Catalog Card No: 2007932762
ISBN: 1-58042-216-0

Visit our web site—www.cardozapub.com—or write for a full list of books and computer strategies.

CARDOZA PUBLISHING
P.O. Box 1500, Cooper Station, New York, NY 10276
Phone (800) 577-WINS
email: cardozapub@aol.com
www.cardozapub.com

CONTENTS

SECTION I
Online Poker Overview

1. INTRODUCTION

It is a brand new world out there. Online poker is hot, and millions of people around the world play it safely on a regular basis. You can play for free on all major sites, a service that's offered to players to get accustomed to online poker—or you can play for real money.

You'll find that playing online poker is just as easy as playing live; in fact it's easier. The software does it all—shuffles and deals the cards, displays betting choices, shows whose turn it is to act and how much is in the pot, makes sure the correct amount is bet, and automatically displays the winning hand at the showdown. And after a bet is placed or a pot is won, the screen displays how much money each player has remaining.

After a minute or two of playing, you may wonder what's so difficult about playing online. To cut the suspense, I'll answer that now: nothing!

In this book, I'm going to show you how to get started in the exciting world of online poker. If you're already familiar with the sites, I'll show you how to improve your play with powerful poker strategies as well as strategies that work specifically for the online game. You'll also learn how to play safely, and most importantly, how to win money.

We'll concentrate on the game of no-limit hold'em, but also cover other games found online—limit hold'em, pot-limit hold'em, seven-card stud, five-card stud, and Omaha. You'll learn how to find and play online tournaments, including satellites and supersatellites for the World Series of Poker and other major events, plus sit-and-gos and online events with million-dollar prize pools. Finally, I'll show you how to take advantage of the many freerolls offered online—tournaments that allow you to play for free, while still being eligible for cash and other prizes! The wave of the future is here. There's a lot of fun to be had online and a lot of money to be made. Let's get started!

2. WHAT DOES ONLINE POKER LOOK LIKE?

Playing online poker is just as easy as playing live poker with your friends. In fact, it's even easier!

But new players ask, "What does online poker look like?" If you're already familiar with playing games on your computer, it's just another game. And if you're new to the online world of gaming, you're in for a lot of fun.

Online poker recreates the experience of a live game without actual opponents sitting around a table in front of you. But online, those opponents *are* there. You just can't see them.

All online poker sites display a graphic of a poker table on your computer screen. Around the table will be representations of players in the form of icons or symbols (two- or three-dimensional representations of a character the player has chosen as his image at the table) or photographs of the actual player (or who that player would like you to believe he or she looks like). These icons, or symbols, vary by poker network, and are commonly called **avatars**. For example, the screenshots on the next page show some avatars from cardozagames.com.

In these graphics, you see players sitting around a table. Each image represents an actual player somewhere in the world who has joined this game. In image "A," we see a table with ten players engaged in a game of hold'em. In image "B," the three characters represented signify that it's a three-player game. The empty seats indicate that no players are active in those spots. Any player from anywhere around the globe, from Russia to Aruba to South Africa, can join in and play at one of the empty seats—just like a live poker game or even a private one among friends.

Full 10-Player Table

3-Player Table

On the screenshots, you also see information showing each player's bankroll, his screen name, and your options for betting, raising, and folding. What you can't see on this screen shot are the ambient sounds that online software makes available. Each site handles this differently; but in general, if you keep your computer's volume on, you'll hear the sounds of chips, bets, and other sounds that emulate the texture of a real poker game and add to the richness of the online poker experience.

When you're online, you'll have a choice of thousands of games to join, with stakes ranging from pennies to hundreds of dollars per bet. And if you're so inclined, there are options to play strictly for fun with no betting at all!

HOW IS ONLINE POKER DIFFERENT FROM LIVE GAMES?

Besides the obvious fact that you can't see your opponents face-to-face like you can when they're seated in front of you, there are differences in playing poker online. For one, the people-reading skills, which are so important in live play, are diminished online because you can't look anyone in the eyes or read their body language. Instead, you have to rely more on pure poker skills, playing cards and situations (just like in live play), but in a purer form because you can't make deductions based on visuals. At the same time, there are still lots of tells specific to online poker, and I've devoted an entire section to them.

But before I go any farther, let me make one thing clear: Poker is poker. If you're playing poker online, it's more or less like playing a live game. You have the same number, order and procedure of betting rounds, the same betting rules, and the best hand will win at the showdown (or the last remaining player will win if all opponents fold before that point). Some games are tight, while others are loose; and you'll encounter aggressive, conservative, tight, and loose players. The same rules and procedures apply to hold'em as to seven-card stud, five-card stud, or the Omaha games.

But while there are similarities, there are differences as well. You have a wide variety of games, limits, tables and, tournaments to choose from at all times. And you can find variations you'd never find in live play, like five-card stud, for instance. For example, you can go to cardozagames.com right now and play this classic poker game. But if you walk into a poker room, good luck. There may not be a single five-card game being spread in a live card room anywhere as you read this.

There are a lot of differences between live and Internet play, and we'll examine those differences in this book. But first, let's look at the advantages of playing poker online, a few of which we've already touched upon.

3. FIFTEEN ADVANTAGES OF ONLINE POKER

If you are new to the world of Internet poker, here are fifteen advantages, compared to live play, that are sure to get you excited about joining the cyberspace craze.

1. PLAY ANYTIME

Anytime, day or night, all you have to do is go to your computer, log on to your poker site of choice, and off you go. You're playing! There is nothing easier than that. It doesn't matter what you're wearing—or not wearing!—or how you look. You don't have to travel to a card room and search for the right game; with thousands of players online at all hours, there is always a game with the right stakes waiting for you. Keep the car in the garage. Save the gas. Just click and go.

2. CONVENIENCE

You can roll out of bed, crawl over to your computer, log on, and you're in a game. It can't get any more convenient than that. Actually, it can. Keep the computer in bed and log in when you turn over. Warning: Any company you keep in bed may not appreciate the competition.

3. GREAT CHOICE OF GAMES

You can find any brand of hold'em on the Internet and for almost any stakes. Limit, no-limit, pot-limit, small stakes, medium stakes, high stakes, penny-ante, free-play, ring games, tournaments, sit-and-gos, satellites, free-money play, shorthanded, heads-up, etc.—you name it, there is a game for you.

4. NO WAITING

Seats are always available online. You'll be in the biggest poker capital of the world—the Internet. Hundreds of sites are just one click away. With endless numbers of choices available, you'll almost always find one with a seat open that exactly suits what you're looking for.

5. YOU SAVE POKER MONEY

There are no dealers, floormen, cocktail waitresses, or runners to tip, and the rakes are lower than in traditional poker rooms. You also incur no expenses getting to or from a game. With all these advantages, you get more bang for your poker buck. That leaves more money on the table for you to keep—or to win.

6. THEY GIVE YOU MONEY TO PLAY!

Did I say they give you money? Yes! Online sites fiercely compete for your business, so they offer free-money bonus deals and other assorted goodies to get you to play on their site. There are other non-cash bonuses sites give you for playing with them—benefits you would not get in live play—so this adds even more value to playing online.

7. IT'S GOOD SOCIAL FUN

Poker fires up that competitive spirit and is a great social outlet as well. You may not be able to see your opponents, but that won't stop you from being able to communicate with them. Just as in a live game, you *can* interact with your tablemates. The chat windows in online sites allow you to type messages back and forth to your fellow players.

8. MAKE FRIENDS AROUND THE WORLD

Internet poker is now a worldwide phenomenon and it is not uncommon to see players at your table from a variety of countries. Like everything else, you eventually strike up friendships. And you never know, you may soon be visiting some of your Internet poker buddies—or receiving them. Many great friendships have started online.

9. IT'S FASTER THAN LIVE GAMES AND GREAT PRACTICE

Online poker moves much faster than regular live games so you get to see lots of hands and situations. You can practice skills that you'll be able to apply to your regular tournament or cash game. And the speed of play—which is typically at least three times as fast as live games (no need to wait while the dealer shuffles, deals, and handles the cards)—makes for less boredom while you wait for good hands to play.

10. PLAY FOR SMALL MONEY, BIG MONEY—OR PLAY FOR FREE

You can play poker for free on pretty much every site; this no-cost feature is a service online poker rooms offer their customers so they can get acclimated to the software and to playing poker online. Or, if you prefer, you can sign up and play for real money, from penny-ante games to games with higher stakes involved.

11. LESS INTIMIDATING THAN LIVE PLAY

When you join a game online, you don't have to be uncomfortable among strangers as you might be in a live game. You don't have to worry about anyone giving you funny looks if you make unusual or poor plays. Like a slot or video poker machine in a casino, you are a faceless player against a computer screen. Many players like that anonymity.

12. YOU CAN PLAY AS A TEAM

If you and a buddy want to enjoy a game together making mutual decisions, you can easily do so without breaking etiquette or ethical codes—as long as you do so playing just one hand. (Playing together on different screens would be collusion, an entirely different thing). You can also bring on a coach to help with decision-making or keep a book by your side as a guide. These are things you can't do in live play.

13. PLAY IN A SMOKE-FREE OR SMOKE-FRIENDLY ENVIRONMENT

Nonsmokers can enjoy the clean smoke-free air of their home without being subjected to the stuffy air of card rooms. And even though many card rooms are smoke-free, smoke from adjacent areas often permeates the air, making the conditions less than ideal. On the other hand, smokers can puff away without offending other players. In either case, as a smoker or nonsmoker, when you're playing at home, you choose the playing conditions.

14. PLAY MULTIPLE GAMES SIMULTANEOUSLY

You can easily play multiple games online at the same time. Experienced online players routinely play four or more games simultaneously and may even compete in a tournament at the same time! Online software allows multiple-table play, which means more action, more fun, and for good players, more profit!

15. IT'S PROFITABLE

Online players are generally weaker than the competitors you'll find in regular cash games, especially at the low-limit games. This makes it very profitable for good players. If you're a really skilled player, it's more than a good way to make money— it's a great way to make a living!

There are many skilled players bringing in more than $100,000 per year playing online poker. In fact, some of the top online players make *millions* of dollars per year! You read that right—millions!

4. SAFETY AND SECURITY ONLINE

The most important consideration in choosing an online poker room is to have a comfort level with the site—that is, to make sure the money you maintain with the online site is safe and secure. In other words, you need to trust a company that you not only can't see with your own eyes but which is likely located continents away.

When you start winning—and that should be your goal—your funds will be kept in the guardianship of the online poker room until you decide to withdraw some or all of it. At that point, you want to be confident that your money gets back to you upon your request. So, yes, trust is your main concern. But the good news is that if you choose a reputable site, your money should be safe.

It's easy to get paranoid about playing for money online. After all, you can't see your opponents and a run of bad luck can have you questioning the integrity of the software.

Here are five reasons why *reputable* online poker sites are safe.

1. ONLINE SITES CANNOT MANIPULATE THE SOFTWARE

Many players are concerned with being cheated by the online software, and with the idea that the Internet poker site can control the cards. This is a possibility, but one so remote and farfetched that you shouldn't worry about it. This won't happen at major sites. Internet sites enjoy no benefit in manipulating the cards. In fact, while altering card values is theoretically possible, practically speaking, it is near impossible.

Businesses like my site, cardozagames.com, and others that are part of a big poker network, have no control over the software whatsoever. We couldn't alter the cards if we wanted to—and believe me, no Internet poker site, no matter how big or small, would change cards if they could (and, as I stated above, they *can't* when they belong to a group where the software is controlled by an outside party). The list of disadvantages for doing so would be long, with the benefits being nil.

2. ONLINE SITES DON'T WANT TO MANIPULATE THE SOFTWARE

The first thing you have to understand to put your mind at ease is that your interests and the online poker rooms are perfectly aligned. The poker operators have one goal—to provide a fair and safe game so players keep playing. They make nothing by you losing money, because that money doesn't go to them! It goes to other players. Online sites profit by keeping the game going. They only make money on the rake, a small amount taken out of every pot as a fee for hosting the game. In fact, it would be detrimental to a site if you got cheated out of your money and stopped playing!

Established Internet poker sites make enormous amounts of money by running legitimate businesses. Should they ever treat a customer in an underhanded way or allow dubious events to occur on their sites, word of mouth on the Internet and the closeness of the poker community would punish the site more harshly than any regulatory commission possibly could. Their players would exit in droves, and if the violations were bad enough, the sites' overall financial health would be in jeopardy. The poker sites have way too much vested in giving you a fair shake to allow shady dealings in their space.

Online sites want to ensure that you're a happy customer who will continue playing with them. Dealing you a fair and honest game is a site's best protection toward that goal. Millions of dollars and years of testing were invested by the software companies to ensure that their software is safe and reliable.

3. YOUR OPPONENTS CANNOT MANIPULATE THE SOFTWARE

Your opponents cannot control the cards you get, nor can they gain access to the hole cards displayed on your computer. Online poker rooms use the same level of security and encryption technology as employed in banking transfers, so the level of protection for your monetary transactions and player information, such as your hole cards, is equally as secure at your online poker room as that enjoyed by financial institutions. Remember, Internet poker software has been tested to death. The puzzle of keeping private information secure has been solved long ago. If you can trust ATM cash machines and online banking, then you can trust the reliability of Internet software sites.

Think of your online security in another way. You're competing at a table where tens or even hundreds of dollars may be at stake on any one hand. Why would a brilliant computer hacker, sophisticated and skilled enough to break into back-level encryption software even think of wasting time at a nickel-and-dime operation when the identical effort can be used to tap into millions of dollars of financial transactions all over the world? In other words, don't worry!

4. THE RANDOM NUMBER GENERATORS KEEP CARDS RANDOM

The distribution of cards dealt to each player online is kept random by software algorithms called random number generators (RNGs). These programs are sophisticated and tested to a point far beyond what could ever be achieved by a hand shuffle. Hands down, you get a much more random shuffle than you'll ever see in a live game (and a more secure one as well). There is no dealer who can manipulate the cards, nor can any player follow the progress of a card as it makes its way through the deck during the shuffling process.

You'll sometimes hear online players complain that their software is dishonest because an opponent got dealt pocket aces two out of three hands, and then he receives pocket kings a few hands later. It happens in live games as well. What's the difference? Nothing. They're just random events. Every day strange things occur in live and online games. You'll notice them more online because of the greater number of hands you'll be dealt each hour, which means more opportunities to witness "unlikely" events. They'll also be more prominent in your mind because they'll feed into the greater amount of paranoia inherent in a situation where you can't physically see the dealer or your opponents.

5. BETTER PROTECTION AGAINST COLLUSION

Because you have secure software transactions and communications does not mean cheating is not possible. However, it's not the online poker rooms you need to be wary of, it's the players, and it can come in the form of collusion. This can occur by multiple players working together against unaware opponents or with an individual having multiple online identities and playing more than one hand. In either case, this *is* cheating.

However, be aware that while it is easier for players to collude online—just like it can happen in any live game—at the same time, it is easier to detect it. The software program keeps all hand histories and can go back and track suspicious behavior from players to determine if there was foul play. Most of the big poker networks have put in place anti-collusion measures and sophisticated software routines to analyze data and determine if there was activity unbecoming of a fair game, plus they maintain 24/7 live monitoring to analyze game and player behavior. The good news is that players can ask to have a player or situation evaluated, and this can all go on behind the scenes with no one knowing who instigated the investigation or suspected players even knowing this is happening. And if colluders are caught, they will be banned from playing, period.

Your best protection, as in any live face-to-face game, is to trust your instincts. If you're ever uncomfortable in a game, switch tables; or if you feel uncomfortable playing on a particular site, then switch sites.

SUMMARY

Your security and peace of mind online is so important, that I'll say this again: It's in a site's best interest to eradicate cheating on any level and provide reliable software, as the most profitable game for a poker site is an honest one. Poker sites have nothing to gain by cheating customers—or allowing cheating—and *everything* to lose. If you choose a reputable casino to play at, you're going to get dealt a fair game online.

But how do you know if the online poker site you're contemplating is the best one for you? Let's look at that now.

5. CHOOSING THE RIGHT SITE

Okay, so you're new to the world of online poker or have been playing awhile and want to make the best choice on where to play. There are five criteria you should consider before making your final choice—or choices, since many players play at more than one site.

In this section, I have laid out, in order of importance, five factors you should consider when picking out an online poker room to play in.

FIVE REASONS TO CHOOSE YOUR POKER SITE
1. Choose a Reputable Site!

There are hundreds of online poker sites available having various degrees of integrity and financial stability. If you're going to be playing online for real money, you'll want to know that your money is in good hands. There have been several instances where players got hung out to dry by online sites run by disreputable people. And note that just because a company is listed on a stock ticker (witness Enron and Anderson) doesn't make your money secure. It comes down to the people who run the business.

The security and safety of your money is your top priority and where your online site does their business banking is your business, too. It could be a concern if your funds are held in questionable offshore banks in third-world countries, where—and it wouldn't be the first time—things could happen.

So how do you play with a site that you know is safe?

Fortunately, there are easy answers. My advice: If you stick to major sites, with reputable people behind it, you shouldn't have too many worries about banking relationships, withdrawing money when you want it, and other basic things you want to take for granted when playing for money online. When you play poker, winning should be the only concern you have. I would suggest avoiding small poker rooms that have the aura of, well, small poker rooms. I am not in a position to list sites that are safe, because obviously I cannot guarantee or vouch for the integrity of anyone else's business other than my own. But the major sites appear to be more secure.

One of the reasons I chose to start cardozagames.com—at the urging of many in the industry—was to bring a steadying and established presence to online poker, and so, in 2007, that is what I did. That is why, at cardozagames.com, we were able to establish secure licensing and banking relationships in the oldest and most conservative venue in the world, the British Commonwealth.

2. You Want Lots of Players!

Before you sign up to an online site, you want to make sure that there are lots of players and games on their network so you can always find a game when you log on. In the industry, we call this *liquidity*. Online poker sites achieve liquidity by joining a poker network that *already* has an abundance of players. That's why my company aligned itself with Playtech, Europe's largest poker network. Rather than going out on our own and offering our players few games to choose from, we made the decision to offer a wide variety of games 24/7.

The major sites good liquidity and will give you action any time, day or night, for the games you want to play. If most of North America is sleeping when you want to play, you may find plenty of action coming out of Europe, Australia or Asia. It really doesn't matter where the players are coming from. On a big site, they'll be there, 24/7, waiting to mix it up with you at the tables.

3. Choose Good Software and Features

You're either paying for fun or you're playing for money, but in either case, you want to be at a site that has a good user interface and *feels* good. Some sites supply extra features that are really advantageous to the user. For example, at cardozagames. com, we offer our customers a rich library of strategy support and exclusive software tools so that our players can improve their game and make money online.

You'll probably enjoy the software at most sites, but it is worth pointing out that you want to be happy with the "feel" of the site you choose.

4. Good Customer Service

Customer service is important to insuring that you enjoy a good experience online. You want to get relatively quick answers to any questions you might have—from major concerns like depositing or withdrawing money, to things like basic features. Of course, it will be hard to tell how effective a poker room's customer support is until you use it, but you'll want to hold your site to a high standard. Again, the only concern you'll want to have online is how best to beat your opponents and take their money, or if you're playing for free, how to maximize your experience.

INSIDER TIP	**LOOK FOR LIQUIDITY!** Before you sign up to an online site, make sure that it has enough players to offer you a wide choice of games around the clock.

5. Loyalty and Deposit Bonuses

To entice new players, online poker rooms offer attractive packages that include cash bonuses worth hundreds of dollars and other similar benefits. To retrieve these bonuses, simply go to a site's homepage (or respond to an ad) and take advantage of the available deals. It's free money you can use on the site, so the bonuses are a great deal.

Some players jump from site to site, taking advantage of the sign-up bonuses. But while site-jumping has its obvious advantages, there are disadvantages as well. Bonus hoppers must continually adjust to new environments and opponents. In addition to rarely having the comfort of a familiar playing environment, and leaving behind online friends, another disadvantage is that bonus hoppers lose out on the free perks given to frequent players. Sites are proactive with bonuses and rewards for their frequent players, part of their efforts to reward good customers. For example, at cardozagames.com, we have set up a program with five levels of VIP rewards to keep our regular players happy.

Satisfied and happy players stay loyal and keep playing, which means rakes continue to get generated for the site. So while there are advantages of getting a deposit bonus as a new player to a site—and you should definitely take advantage of these as a first-time player—there is a lot to be said to sticking with a site where you are comfortable and getting rewarded for staying loyal. You could make a good case that a comfortable playing environment gives you the best chances for success.

SECTION II
How to Play Poker

1. INTRODUCTION

Playing poker on the Internet has made life easy for modern-day poker players. With just a few clicks of your mouse, you can get in on the action, too. You can try out the free money games to get accustomed to playing online, or if you're ready for real-money play, you can compete for winnings as soon as you get money into your account.

With automatic and random card "shuffling," you'll find that online poker moves much faster than live poker; so it's a great place to hone skills for your regular tournament or cash game, and of course, to enjoy the game any time you want. And if you're a winning player, more hands per hour mean more money won!

In this section, we'll cover the basics of playing poker, whether played live or online, so you can sit down and play poker with complete confidence. If you're unfamiliar with the rules and procedures of poker, one quick reading here and you'll be on your way to this great game and perhaps lots of profits!

2. OVERVIEW

Poker is a betting game requiring two or more players. It is played with a standard pack of fifty-two cards consisting of thirteen ranks, ace through king, in each of four suits (hearts, clubs, diamonds, spades). The ace is the best and highest card, followed in descending order by the king, queen, jack, 10, 9, 8, 7, 6, 5, 4, 3 and then the **deuce** or 2, which is the lowest ranked card. The king, queen and the jack are known as **picture cards** or **face cards**.

The four suits in poker have no basic value in the determination of winning hands.

Cards are referred to in writing by the following commonly used symbols: ace (A), king (K), queen (Q), jack (J), and all others directly by their numerical value, 10, 9, 8, 7, 6, 5, 4, 3, and 2.

THE FOUR SUITS

clubs   diamonds   hearts   spades

When the cards are held together in various combinations, they form hands of different strengths. These are called **hand rankings** or **poker rankings**.

There are many variations of poker, but they all have these four things in common:

1. Players receive an equal number of cards to start.

2. There will be a wager after these cards are received; players that match the wager can continue playing the hand, players that don't match the wager will sit out. You have to pay to play!

3. More cards are usually dealt after the first round of play, with players having an option to wager more money following each round of cards.

4. The winner of each hand will be the player with the highest ranked hand or the last one remaining in play (because his opponents have opted out of the hand).

Each player in poker plays by himself and for himself alone against all other players. Playing partners is illegal and is considered cheating.

OBJECT OF THE GAME

Your goal in poker is to win the money in the **pot**, the accumulation of bets and antes in the center of the table. You can win in two ways.

The first way is to have the highest ranking hand at the **showdown**—the final act in poker, where all active players' hands are revealed to see who has the best one. The second way is to be the last player remaining when all other players have dropped out of play. When this occurs, there is no showdown, and you automatically win the pot.

3. TYPES OF POKER GAMES

If you're new to poker, your choice of games can be confusing. Not only do you have variations such as hold'em, Omaha, seven-card stud, five-card stud and variations within these, but there is high poker, low poker and high-low poker. Then there are cash games and tournaments, as well as limit, no-limit, and pot-limit betting structures.

Huh? How do you make sense of them all? Here's a down and dirty guide so you can understand all your choices.

BASIC GAME FORMATS

Poker can be played in two basic forms—as cash games or in a tournament format. Let's take a quick look at each one.

Cash Games

In a **cash game**, the chips you play with represent real money. If you go broke, you can always dig in to your pocket for more money. If you buy in for $100, you get $100 worth of chips in return. If you build it up to $275, you can quit and convert your chips to cash anytime you want. Your goal in a cash game is to win as much money as you can, or if things go against you, to minimize losses.

Tournaments and Sit-and-gos

In a **tournament**, every player starts with an equal number of chips and plays until one player holds them all. Your goal in a tournament is to survive as long as you can. At the very least, you want to survive long enough to earn prizes, usually money, and in the best case scenario, to win it all, become the champion, and win the biggest prize. As players lose their chips, they are eliminated from the tournament. Unlike a cash game, where the chips are the equivalent of cash money, **tournament chips** are only valuable in the tournament itself and have no cash value.

Sit-and-gos are typically one-table tournaments that begin as soon as a table is filled; there is no scheduled starting time. Cash prizes are typically paid to the top three places—50% for the winner, 30% for second place, and 20% for third place. Online sit-and-gos often use the initials *SNG*. There are also two-table SNGs and occasionally, three-table ones as well.

BETTING STRUCTURES

Poker has three different types of betting structures: limit, pot-limit, and no-limit. These structures don't change the basic way the games are played, only the amount of money that can be bet. The big difference between the three structures is the strategy. The amount you can bet changes the hands that you should play, when you should play them, and how much you should risk in any given situation.

Limit Poker

In **limit** poker, all bets are divided into a two-tier structure, such as 50¢/$1, $1/$2, $3/$6, and $5/$10, with the larger limit bets being exactly double the lower limit. On the preflop and flop, all bets and raises must be at the lower limit, and on the turn and river, all bets double and are made at the higher limit. In a $5/$10 limit game, for example, when the lower limit of betting is in effect, all bets and raises must be in $5 increments. When the upper range is in effect, all bets and raises must be in $10 increments.

In the sections on the individual games, we will go over exactly when the upper level of betting comes into effect and how that works.

No-Limit Poker

No-limit is the exciting no-holds barred style of poker played in the World Series of Poker main event and seen on television by millions weekly. The prevailing feature of no-limit poker is that you can bet any amount up to what you have in front of you on the table *anytime* it is your turn. That exciting all-in call signals a player's intention to put all his chips on the line. No-limit is usually associated with Texas hold'em, but this style of betting can be played in any variation.

Pot-Limit Poker

Pot-limit is most often associated with hold'em and Omaha, though this betting structure, like no-limit, can be played with any poker variation. The minimum bet allowed in pot-limit is set in advance while the maximum bet allowed is defined by the size of the *pot*. For example, if $75 is currently in the pot, then $75 is the maximum bet allowed.

The pot sizes in pot-limit quickly escalate to large amounts. Like no-limit, this betting structure is not for the timid.

HAND RANKINGS

Poker is typically played as **high poker**, that is, the player with the best and highest five-card combination at the showdown wins the money in the pot. But there are also variations where the low hand wins, and some, where players compete for both ends of the spectrum—the best high hand and the best low hand.

Of course, in each variation, the pot can also be won by a player when all of his opponents fold their hands at any point before the showdown, leaving one player alone to claim the pot—even though he may not actually have held the best hand!

High Poker

The best poker hand you can hold is the royal flush, followed by a straight flush, four of a kind, full house, flush, straight, three of a kind, two pair, one pair, and high card hand. The order in which cards are dealt or how they are displayed is irrelevant to the final value of the hand. For example, 7-7-K-A-5 is equivalent to A-K-7-7-5.

Poker hands are ranked the way they are because of one

cold, hard fact: The more difficult it is, statistically speaking, to be dealt a particular poker hand in five cards, the higher it ranks on the scale of poker hands. Note that all poker hands eventually consist of five cards, regardless of the variation played.

High-Card Hands

A hand containing five unmatched cards, that is, lacking any of the combinations shown below, is valued by its highest ranking card. The hand, 3-9-K-7-10, would be called a "king-high" hand. When the highest ranking cards are identical, the next highest untied card wins. A-K-J-10-4 beats A-K-J-3-2.

One Pair

Two cards of equal rank and three unmatched cards. Example: 5-5-8-J-K. If two players are competing with one-pair hands, then the higher ranked of the pairs—aces highest, deuces lowest—wins the pot. And if two players have the same pair, then the highest side card would be used to determine the higher-ranking hand. 5-5-A-7-6 beats 5-5-K-Q-J, since the ace is a higher kicker (unpaired side card) than the king.

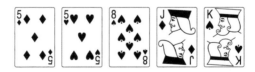

Two Pair

Two pairs and an unmatched card. Example: 6-6-J-J-2. The highest pair of competing two-pair hands will win, or if the top pair is tied, then the second pair. If both pairs are equivalent, then the fifth card decides the winner. K-K-3-3-6 beats J-J-8-8-Q and K-K-2-2-A, but loses to K-K-3-3-9.

Three of a Kind

Three cards of equal rank and two unmatched cards. Also called **trips** or a **set**. Example: Q-Q-Q-7-J. If two players hold a set, the higher ranked set will win, and if both players hold an equivalent set, then the highest odd card determines the winner. 7-7-7-4-2 beats 5-5-5-A-K, but loses to 7-7-7-9-5.

Straight

Five cards of mixed suits in sequence, but it may not wrap around the ace. For example, Q-J-10-9-8 of mixed suits is a straight, but Q-K-A-2-3 is not—it's simply an ace-high hand. If two players hold straights, the higher straight card at the top end of the sequence will win. J-10-9-8-7 beats 5-4-3-2-A but would tie another player holding J-10-9-8-7.

Flush

Five cards of the same suit. Example: K-10-9-5-3, all in diamonds. If two players hold flushes, the player with the highest card wins or if they're equal, then the highest untied card determines the winner. Suits have no relevance. Thus, Q-J-7-5-4 of diamonds beats Q-J-4-3-2 of spades.

Full House

Three of a kind and a pair. Example: 5-5-5-9-9. If two players hold full houses, the player with the higher three of a kind wins. J-J-J-8-8 beats 7-7-7-A-A.

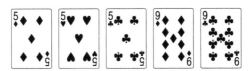

Four of a Kind

Four cards of equal rank and an odd card. Also called **quads**. Example: K-K-K-K-3. If two players hold quads, the higher ranking quad will win the hand. K-K-K-K-3 beats 7-7-7-7-A and K-K-K-K-2.

Straight Flush

Five cards in sequence, all in the same suit. Example: 7-6-5-4-3, all in spades. If two straight flushes are competing, the one with the highest card wins.

Royal Flush

The A-K-Q-J-10 of the same suit, the best hand possible. No royal flush is higher than another.

LOW POKER

In **low poker**, the ranking of hands is the opposite to that of high poker, with the lowest hand being the most powerful and the highest hand being the least powerful. There are two varieties of low poker games: ace-to-five and deuce-to-seven.

In **ace-to-five**, the ace is considered the lowest and therefore most powerful card. The hand 5-4-3-2-A is the best low total possible with 6-4-3-2-A and 6-5-3-2-A being the next two best hands. Straights and flushes don't count against low hands.

In **deuce-to-seven** low poker, also known as **Kansas City lowball**, the 2 is the lowest and best card and the ace is the highest and worst. The hand 7-5-4-3-2 is the best possible hand, followed by 7-6-4-3-2 and 7-6-5-3-2. In this variation, unlike ace-to-five, straights and flushes count as high so you don't want to end up with 7-6-5-4-2 all in hearts, or 8-7-6-5-4.

HIGH-LOW POKER

In **high-low** poker (and its variant, **high-low 8-or-better**), players compete for either the highest-ranking or lowest-ranking hand, with the best of each claiming half the pot—with some restrictions, which we'll go into below. The best high hand and the best low hand split the pot, or if one player is fortunate enough to have the best high and low, he'll claim it all or **scoop**.

High-low games are sometimes played with a **qualifier**, a requirement that a player must have five unpaired cards of 8 or less to win the low end of the pot. If no player has an 8-or-better qualifier, then the best high hand will win the entire pot. For example, if the best low at the table is 9-6-5-4-2, then there is no qualified low hand and the best high hand will win the entire pot. This version of high-low is called **8-or-better**.

4. THE BASICS OF ONLINE POKER

Poker can be played with as few as two players to as many as the 52-card deck can support. Online, you can plays **heads-up**, with just you against another player, **short-handed** at tables that hold six players maximum, or in a full **ring games** at tables seating eight or ten players. The bigger tables may not always play as full ring games. If they have empty seats, you could be playing six or seven-handed or even heads-up at a full capacity table that isn't filled.

But online, if you don't like the table you're playing at, either because of too few players, or your opponents, you can easily switch to another table and find a game more to your liking. That's one of the great things about playing poker online as opposed to live games. There are a lot of choices.

A **button** is utilized to designate the dealer's imaginary position in hold'em and Omaha. It will rotate around the table, one spot at a time in clockwise fashion so that each player has a chance to enjoy the advantages of acting last.

BUYING IN TO A GAME

To get chips online, you take money from your account and designate the amount that will be used for the game you'll play. It's just like taking money out of your wallet and putting it on a table during a cash game. You take out what you want to risk at the game, and leave the rest tucked away.

This exchange of cash for chips is called a **buy-in** and is done when you join a table. An easy-to-use screen will ask you how much you wish to bring to the table, you enter the amount, click "Enter," "Okay," "Yes" or whatever the appropriate key, and you've got your table buy-in ready to go. Of course, first you'll need to have money deposited in your account.

MANDATORY STARTING BETS

In poker, one or more players are typically required to put a bet into the pot before the cards are dealt. There are two types of mandatory bets: blinds and antes. **Blind bets**, or **blinds**, are used in hold'em, Omaha, and some draw variations. They are generally required of the first two players to the left of the dealer position. An **ante**, also known as a **sweetener**, is a uniform bet placed into the pot by all players before the cards are dealt. The sizes of the blinds and antes will be clearly displayed for each table you contemplate joining.

Players will frequently play forcefully in the early going, hoping to force opposing players out of the pot to pick up the antes and blinds without going further into a hand. Where there are blinds, as in hold'em and Omaha, this is called **stealing the blinds**. In ante games, such as seven-card stud, it is called **stealing the antes**.

Antes or blinds must be placed into the pot before the cards are dealt. This will be done before each deal, with the relevant amount deducted from each players' bankroll.

THE PLAY OF THE GAME

When a new hand is ready to be dealt, the software automatically distributes cards starting with the player situated on the immediate left of the blinds. Cards will be dealt clockwise, one at a time, until each player has received the requisite number of cards for the poker variation being played. Online, this will happen rapidly, or the software might display all the dealt cards simultaneously. In either case, it amounts to the identical thing.

Like the dealing of the cards, play always proceeds in a clockwise direction. The first round begins with the player sitting to the immediate left of the blinds, the dealer, or, in stud games, depending upon the variation, with either the high- or low-card hand opening play. Play will continue around the table, until each player in turn has acted.

In later rounds, the first player to act will vary depending on the poker variation being played. We'll cover the particulars of play under the sections on the games themselves.

THE PLAYER'S OPTIONS

When it is your turn to play, the following options, which apply to all forms of poker, are available to you:

1. **Bet:** Put chips into the pot, that is, wager money if no player has done so before you.

2. **Call:** Match a bet if one has been placed before your turn.

3. **Raise:** Increase the size of a current bet such that opponents, including the original bettor, must put additional money into the pot to stay active in a hand.

4. **Fold:** Give up your cards and opt out of play if a bet is due and you do not wish to match it. This forfeits your chance of competing for the pot.

5. **Check:** Stay active in a hand without making a bet and risking chips. This is only possible if no bets have been made.

The first three options—bet, call, and raise—are all a form of putting chips at risk in hopes of winning the pot. Once chips are bet and due, you must match that bet to continue playing for the pot or you must fold. Checking is not an option. If no chips are due, you can stay active without cost by checking.

If a bet has been made, each active player—one who has not folded—is faced with the same options: call, fold, or raise.

Once a bet has been made, it no longer belongs to the bettor; it becomes the property of the pot, the communal collection of money that is up for grabs by all active players.

Betting continues in a round until the last bet or raise is called by all active players, at which point the betting round is over. A player may not raise his own bet when his betting turn comes around. He may raise only another player's bet or raise.

THE REASON YOU MAKE BETS

You'll make bets for one of three reasons:

1. You feel your hand has enough strength to win and you want to induce opponents to put more money into the pot.

2. You want to force opponents out of the pot so that the field is narrowed, since fewer players increase your chances of winning.

3. You want to induce all your opponents to fold so that you can win the pot uncontested.

MINIMUM AND MAXIMUM BETS: LIMIT POKER

The minimum and maximum bets in limit games are strictly regulated according to the preset limits. For example, $3/$6 and $5/$10 are two common limits in live games, though online, there are lots of choices. The number of raises allowed in a round is also restricted, usually limited to three or four total according to the house rules. In other words, if there is a three-raise limit and the action goes bet, raise, reraise, and reraise, the raising would be **capped**. No more raises would be allowed for that round.

The exception to this rule may come into play when players are heads-up, in which case, on some sites, there is no cap to the number of raises that can be made. (Note: Many sites still maintain the three-raise cap, even in heads-up play.)

MINIMUM AND MAXIMUM BETS: NO-LIMIT POKER

In no-limit cash games and tournaments, there is generally no cap to the number of raises allowed. There is also no limit to how high a bet or raise can be. Players may raise as often as they like and for all their chips.

The minimum bet in no-limit must be at least the size of the big blind while the minimum raise must be at least equal to the size of the previous bet or raise in the round. For example, a $10 bet can be raised $30 more to make it $40 total. If a succeeding player reraises, he would have to make it at least $30 more—since that is the size of the last raise—and would place $70 total into the pot.

BETTING ETIQUETTE

It is improper and illegal to discuss your hand or another player's hand while a game is in progress. This policy will be strictly enforced online as it amounts to interfering with the fair play of a hand. It is also very poor form to criticize other players' strategy decisions, no matter how misguided they appear to be. If you think an opponent plays poorly, then that's good news for you: go win his chips. But do be respectful of these rules and your fellow players.

TABLE STAKES, TAPPED OUT PLAYERS, SIDE POTS

You may only bet or call bets up to the amount of money you have on the table. This is called **table stakes** and is equally enforced online and in live play. You are not allowed to withdraw additional money from your account (and won't be able to anyway) while a hand is in progress. Getting extra cash or chips is permissible only *before* the cards are dealt.

For example, if the bet is $25 and you only have $10 at the table, you may only call for $10. The remaining $15 and all future monies bet during this hand—except for bets by opponents to equal the $10 called by the tapped-out player—

would be separated into a **side pot**. A player who has no more table funds from which to bet is **tapped-out**.

A tapped-out player will still receive cards until the showdown and play for the **main pot**, however, he can no longer bet in this hand and has no interest in the side pot. The other active players can continue to bet against each other for the money in the side pot in addition to remaining in competition for the main pot with the tapped-out player.

At the showdown, if the tapped-out player has the best hand, he receives only the money in the main pot. The side pot will be won by the player holding the best hand among those who were competing for that pot. Should a non-tapped-out player hold the overall best hand, he wins both the original pot and the side pot. If only one opponent remains when a player taps out, then there is no more betting, and cards are played out until the showdown, where the best hand wins.

ALL-IN WAGERS: LIMIT POKER

In limit games play, an all-in wager of less than half the bet for that round will be treated as just a call (and not a raise). It does not reopen the action for any subsequent player who has already acted on their hand that round. Subsequent players who have already acted and are facing less than half a bet can fold or call that wager. They may not raise.

An all-in wager of half a bet or more, but still below the full amount, is treated as a full bet and considered a raise for betting purposes. A subsequent player can fold, call or make a full raise and any player, who had already acted prior to the "all in" bet, also has the full range of options available to him.

ALL-IN WAGERS: NO-LIMIT POKER

In no-limit or pot-limit poker, an "all-in" raise that is less than the bet or raise of the previous player does not reopen the action for players who have already acted on their hands. Any raise that is below the amount needed for a legitimate raise will be considered a call for betting purposes. Only players still to act in the round will receive a full set of options. All wagers must be at least the size of the previous bet or raise in any round unless a player is going "all in."

THE RAKE

Online poker rooms get a small cut of the action, called a **rake**, as its fee for hosting the game. The rake is usually between 0% and 5% of each total pot, typically with a cap of $3 per pot. Rakes are often not charged if a hand ends before the flop is seen. For example, on cardozagames.com, we maintain a rake policy of "No flop, no drop."

5. TEXAS HOLD'EM

Texas hold'em, or **hold'em** as the game is more commonly known, is the hot game it seems *everyone* is playing. We'll go over all the basics of play for this great variation so you can step right in and join the very exciting world of online poker. You'll learn how to play the limit, no-limit, pot-limit and tournament versions and then how to put all the pieces together and walk away with money in your pocket.

Let's get started!

OVERVIEW

Your final five-card hand in hold'em will be made up of the best five-card combination of the seven total cards available to you. These include the **board**, five cards dealt face-up in the middle of the table, cards which are shared by all players, and your **pocket cards** or **hole cards**, two cards dealt face-down that can be used by you alone. For example, your final hand could be composed of your two pocket cards and three cards from the board, one pocket card and four from the board, or simply all five board cards.

At the beginning of a hand, each player is dealt two face-down cards. Then each player gets a chance to exercise his betting options. Next, three cards are dealt simultaneously on the table for all players to share. This is called the **flop**, and it is followed by another round of betting. A fourth board card, called the **turn**, is then dealt, and it too is followed by a round of betting. One final community card is dealt in the center of the table, making five total. This is the **river**. If two or more players remain in the hand, it is followed by the fourth and final betting round.

When all bets have concluded, there is the **showdown**, in which the highest ranking hand in play wins the pot.

HOW TO READ YOUR HOLD'EM HAND

You have all seven cards available to form your final five-card hand—any combination of your two hole cards and the five cards from the board. You can even use all five board cards. Let's look at an example.

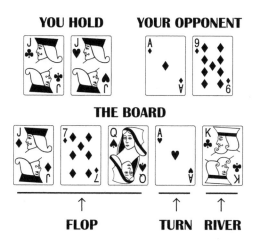

Your best hand, three jacks, is made using your two pocket cards and one jack from the board. This beats your opponent's pair of aces, formed with one card from his hand and one from the board. In both instances, the other cards are not relevant.

If the river card, the last card turned up on the board, had been a K♦ instead of a K♣, your opponent would have a diamond flush (formed with his two pocket diamonds and the three diamonds on the board), which would beat your set of jacks.

THE PLAY OF THE GAME

All play and strategy in hold'em depends upon the position of the **button**, which is a small disk, typically plastic and labeled "Dealer." The player who has the button in front of him, who is also known as the button, will have the advantage of acting last in every round of betting except for the preflop. After each hand is completed, the disk will rotate clockwise to the next player.

The player immediately to the left of the button is called the **small blind** and the one to his left is called the **big blind**. These two players are required to post bets, called **blinds**, before the cards are dealt.

The Button and the Blinds

The big blind is typically the same size as the lower bet in a limit structure, so if you're in a $3/$6 game, the big blind would be $3 and in a $5/$10 game, it would be $5. The small blind will either be half the big blind in games where the big blind evenly divides to a whole dollar, or two-thirds of the big blind when it doesn't. For example, the small blind might be $2 in a $3/$6 game and $10 in a $15/$30 game. Online, because it is simple to divide the dollar amounts and use change, small blinds might be in broken dollar amounts, such as $2.50 in a $5/$10 game.

In no-limit cash games, the blind amounts are preset and remain constant throughout the game. In tournaments, however, the blinds steadily increase as the event progresses, forcing players to play boldly to keep up with the greater costs of the blinds.

ORDER OF BETTING

Play always proceeds clockwise around the table. On the preflop, the first betting round, the first player to the left of the big blind goes first. He can call the big blind to stay in competition for the pot, raise, or fold. Every player following him has the same choices: call, raise, or fold. The last player to act on the preflop is the big blind. If no raises have preceded his turn, the big blind can either end the betting in the round by calling, or he can put in a raise. However, if there are any raises in the round, the big blind and other remaining players must call or raise these bets to stay active, or they must fold.

On the other betting rounds—the flop, turn and river—the first active player to the button's left will go first and the player on the button will go last. If the button has folded, the player sitting closest to his right will act last. When all bets and raises have been met on the flop and turn, or if all players check, then the next card will be dealt. On the river, after all betting action is completed, players will reveal their cards to see who has the best hand.

Betting in a round stops when the last bet or raise has been called and no bets or raises are due any player. Players cannot raise their own bets or raises.

At any time before the showdown, if all opponents fold, then the last active player wins the pot.

<table>
<tr><td>INSIDER TIP</td><td>**PLAYING TIP**
Never fold when you're in the big blind position if the pot has not been raised—there is no cost to play and you can see the flop for free.</td></tr>
</table>

SAMPLE GAME

Let's follow the action in a sample $3/$6 limit game with ten players so that you can see how hold'em is played. Note that a no-limit game would proceed *exactly* like the sample limit hold'em game shown below. The only difference is that players could bet or raise any amount greater than the minimum allowed, up to all their chips, when it is their turn.

Once the cards are dealt, the player to the big blind's left acts first. He has the option of calling the $3 big blind bet, raising it $3 more, or folding. Checking is not an option on the preflop as there is already a bet on the table—the $3 big blind bet. Let's say that the first two players fold. The next player is faced with the same decisions: call, raise, or fold. He calls for $3. Since this is a $3/$6 game, all bets and raises in this round *must* be in $3 increments. The next three players fold. The following player raises $3, making it $6 total—the $3 call plus the $3 raise.

It is the button's turn, the player sitting in the dealer position. He thinks about his cards and calls the $6. Now it is up to the small blind. The small blind has already put in $2 so he must put in $4 more to play. If there had been no raise, it would cost him just $1 more to meet the $3 big blind bet and stay active.

The small blind folds and the big blind considers reraising the raiser, but instead just calls the $3 raise. Play now moves back to the original caller. Since he has only put $3 into the pot, he must meet the $3 raise to stay in the hand. He calls and since all bets and raises have been matched, the round is over. We'll see the flop four-handed.

Note that the big blind always has the option to raise on the preflop, even if all opponents just call. The screen will display the playing options—CALL, RAISE, FOLD—on the big blind's turn. If there had been no raises and the big blind calls, the preflop betting is finished for the round. If the big blind raises, then the other active players must meet that raise to stay active.

If all players fold on the preflop, the big blind wins the hand by default.

THE FLOP

On the flop, the first active player to the button's left goes first. Since the small blind has folded, it is the big blind's turn. There are no bets that have to be met—the forced first round blind bet only occurs on the preflop—so the big blind may check or bet. (There is no reason to fold, which would be foolish, as it costs nothing to stay active.)

The action goes as follows: the big blind checks, the next player checks, the original preflop raiser checks, and it is now up to the button. He pushes $3 into the pot forcing the other three players to call the $3 if they want to see another card. The big blind, who originally checked this round, is the next active player. He must call or raise this bet to continue with the hand, or he must fold. He decides to call for $3 and the other two players fold. Since all bets have been called, betting is complete for the round.

We're now heads-up, the big blind versus the button.

THE TURN

On the turn, betting moves to the upper limit, so now all bets and raises are in $6 increments. A fourth community card will appear on the screen. The big blind, being the first active player on the button's left, goes first. He checks. The button checks as well. Since all active players checked, the betting round is over.

THE RIVER AND THE SHOWDOWN

A fifth and final community card is turned over and placed next to the other four cards in the center of the table. Players now have five community cards along with their two pocket cards to form their final five card hand. There is one final round of betting.

The big blind goes first and leads out with a $6 bet. The button calls, and that concludes the betting since the big blind cannot raise his own bet. We now have the showdown. The big blind turns over K-Q, which combines with a board of K-Q-10-7-5 for two pair of kings and queens. The button's K-10 also gives him two pair led by kings, but his second pair is tens. The big blind has the superior hand and wins the money in the pot. Those winnings will automatically be transferred into his table bankroll. So if a player finishes a hand with $226 and wins $44, he would now have a total of $270.

6. SEVEN-CARD STUD

Seven-card stud's three main variations—high, low, and high-low—pack five exciting betting rounds into play. In each variation, players form their best five-card combination out of the seven dealt to produce their final hands.

Players will receive a total of seven cards if they play through to the end. After the first three cards are dealt (two **face-down**, or **closed**, and one **face-up**, or **open**), the first betting round commences. The following three cards—the fourth, fifth and sixth—are dealt open, one at a time to each active player, with a betting round accompanying each card. The last card, the seventh, comes "down and dirty," that is, face-down.

All players who have not folded now hold three hole cards and four open cards. A final round of betting follows the seventh card, and then the showdown occurs with the best hand (or hands, as may be the case in high-low) claiming the pot. In each variation of seven-card stud, a player can also win the pot before the showdown by forcing out all opponents through bets and raises that opponents won't match.

In **seven-card high stud**, the highest ranking hand at the showdown wins the pot. In **seven-card low stud** (also called **razz**), the lowest hand claims the gold. And in **seven-card stud high-low** (and its variant, **seven card stud 8-or-better**), players vie for either the highest-ranking or lowest-ranking hand, with the best of each claiming half the pot—with some restrictions, which we'll go into.

SEVEN-CARD STUD HIGH
The Ante
Before the cards are dealt, each player will contribute an ante to the pot. The ante might be anywhere from 10 percent to 25 percent of the full lower tier bet, depending upon the game.

Third Street and the Bring-In
The player holding the lowest open card must make the **bring-in**, the forced opening bet which will start the action on **third street**, the first round of betting—so named for the three cards that each player holds. The bring-in amount will be 25 percent to 50 percent of the size of the smaller bet in a limit game. For example, in a $3/$6 game online, the forced bring-in might be 90¢ or even $1.50, depending upon the rules established for that table. In a $2/$4 game, the forced bring-in might be 60¢ or $1. (Usually the bring-in is greater than the ante but smaller than the full bet.)

The bring-in bettor may also bet the full amount of the $3 if he chooses to—but no more than the maximum bet allowed for this round, in this example, $3.

If two players have identically ranked cards, the player with the lower-ranked suit plays first. For this purpose only, the suits are ranked alphabetically, with clubs being the lowest, followed by diamonds, hearts, and spades. For example, if the lowest ranked open cards are the 3♣ and the 3♥, the 3♣ makes the bring-in bet.

The first player to the bring-in's left goes next, and has four choices: He must either *call* the bring-in, **complete** the bet, that is, bring it up to the lower limit of the betting structure (so if it's a $3/$6 game with a 90¢ bring-in, then he must put in $2.10 to make it $3), *raise* the completed bring-in (make it $6—a $3 call plus a $3 raise), or *fold*. Note that completing the bring-in is not considered a raise and that a player cannot raise an uncompleted bring-in. Once a player completes the bring-in, subsequent players need only call that bet, in this example, the $3. They could also raise $3 to $6, or fold.

Play will move around the table until all bets and raises have been called. Or the betting will end right there if no player chooses to call the bring-in, giving the opener the pot. Like all other forms of cardroom or online poker, there is no checking on the first betting round. You either put money into the pot, or get out of the hand.

All bets and raises in this first betting round are at the lower limit of the betting tier. So if you're playing a $1/$2 game, all bets would be $1 while in a $5/$10 game, all bets would be $5. If a player wants to raise the completed bring-in in a $1/$2 game, it would be by $1 more, making it $2 to the next player, and in a $5/$10 game, that raise would be for $5.

Fourth Street

When third street betting is completed, each active player receives a face-up card. Everyone now holds a total of four cards, two open and two closed. Play in this round, called **fourth street**, and all the following rounds, begins with the highest ranking open hand and moves clockwise around the table. When two or more players hold identically ranked cards, the player closest to the dealer's left plays first. If players held K-K, A-Q and 4-4, the pair of kings would lead off the betting.

Beginning on fourth street and continuing through the last betting round, the first bettor to act may check since there is no forced bet to meet. All bets and raises on fourth street are in the lower limit unless an open pair shows on board, in which case players may elect to open with a bet from the upper limit of the betting. (If this double bet is made, all subsequent players must call and raise at that level.) Thus, on fourth street in a $5/$10 game, bets would be $5, unless an open pair forms on board, in which case $10 could be bet.

Fifth and Sixth Street

Once fourth street betting is concluded, another open card is dealt to each active player. This round is called **fifth street**. All bets and raises on this round and in the following two rounds, are in the upper tier of the betting limit. In a $1/$2 game, bets and raises would be $2, in a $3/$6 games, $6, and in a $5/$10 game, $10. This next betting round is called **sixth street** and is played in the same fashion as fifth street.

Seventh Street

Seventh street is the final betting round. Each remaining player receives his seventh and final card face-down. There is a round of betting, which is followed by the showdown if two or more players remain.

SEVEN-CARD STUD HIGH-LOW

The main difference between high-low stud and the high version is that you're actually playing for two parts of the pot: half the pot goes to the player holding the best high hand and the other half goes to the player with the best low. Or if one player is fortunate enough to have the best high *and* low, he'll claim it all. The only other difference is that there is no option to make a double bet on fourth street if an open pair shows on board.

All other playing procedures for seven-card stud high and high-low are the same—the low card brings it in on third street, there are five betting rounds, and it's "cards-speak" at the river.

RAZZ

Seven-card stud played for low only is also called razz. The best ranking low hand at the river will be the winner. The lowest and best hand, called a **wheel** or **bicycle**, is A-2-3-4-5 with the second-best hand being A-2-3-4-6. Like the high version of the game, each player gets three cards to start and there are five betting rounds. On third street, the bring-in is made by the highest ranking card (not the lowest as in the high and high-low versions), and thereafter, the lowest ranking hand starts the betting. Straights and flushes do not count against the low ranking of a hand, thus 2-3-4-5-6 all in hearts, is simply a 6-5 low, not a straight or a flush, and it would beat the 7-5 hand of A-3-4-5-7 in mixed suits.

7. FIVE-CARD STUD

Five-card stud is the classic old-style Western poker variation making a comeback through online sites like cardozagames.com. It had all but disappeared from popular play until the advent of online poker. Although it is still not played much, you can find some games online and enjoy one of the simplest forms of poker to play.

Players that play to the river will receive a total of five cards, four **face up** or **open**, for all players to view, and one face down, with the highest-ranking five cards winning the pot. There is no board like hold'em with which you share cards or replenishment as in draw poker. You get five cards total; that's it.

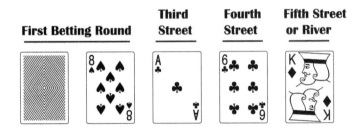

First Betting Round	Third Street	Fourth Street	Fifth Street or River

Here is how the game is played.

THE ANTE

Before the cards are dealt, each player will be required to post an **ante**, a forced bet that gets the action started. For example, in a $4/$8 game, each player might be required to post a 25¢ ante. If eight players are involved in the game, the pot will contain $2 worth of antes. In smaller limit games, like 10¢/20¢, antes may be proportionately higher, for example 5¢, and sometimes the micro-limit games may have no ante at all.

SECOND STREET AND THE BRING-IN

Each player starts with two cards, one face-down and one face-up. The player holding the lowest open card will make the **bring-in**, the forced opening bet that will start the action on the first round of betting. It is usually equal to either one-fourth or one-half of the smaller bet in the two-tier structure. In a $2/$4 game, 50¢ or $1 might be the bring-in; in a $4/$8 game, it might be $1 or $2. He may also complete the bet, bring it up to the full amount of the lower tier, for example, he may make it $2 in a $2/$4 game.

Like seven-card stud, if two players have identically ranked cards, the player with the lower-ranked suit plays first. For this purpose only, the suits are ranked alphabetically, with clubs being the lowest, followed by diamonds, hearts, and spades.

The first player to the bring-in's left goes next, and he must either call the bring-in, complete it, that is, bring it up to the lower limit of the betting structure (so if it's a $2/$4 game with a $1 bring-in, then he must raise $1 to make it $2), raise the completed bring-in, or fold. Play will move around the table until all bets and raises have been called. Or it will end right there if no player chooses to call the bring-in, giving the original bring-in bettor the pot. There is no checking on this round.

THIRD STREET

After all bets have been completed in the first betting round, each remaining player—those who have not folded—will receive a second face-up card. Each player now holds three cards, two up and one down. The second round of betting, called **third street**, begins with the best open hand and moves clockwise around the table. When two or more players hold identically ranked cards, the player closest to the dealer's left plays first. If players showed K-J, A-3, and 7-7 on the board, the pair of sevens would act first since it is the highest-ranking open hand.

If two players happen to be tied for the best open hand, then the player closest to the dealer will act first.

Since there is no forced bring-in on third street (or on the following rounds), the first player to act may check or bet as he desires. Betting on this round, as on the previous round, will be in the lower tier of the betting range, unless an open pair shows on board, in which case players may elect to open with a bet from the upper limit of the betting. So if it's a $2/$4 game, all bets and raises must be in $2 increments. However, if there is an open pair on board, $4 may be bet. (Once a double bet is made, subsequent raises in the round must be at the double-bet level, in this example, $4.)

FOURTH STREET

After third-street betting is completed, assuming two or more players remain to contest the pot, a third open card is dealt to each active bettor, giving each player a total of four cards. On this round, called **fourth street**, and the following one, all bets and raises will be at the higher amount, for example, $4 in a $2/$4 game, and $10 in a $5/$10 game.

FIFTH STREET AND THE SHOWDOWN

If two or more players remain to contest the pot, a fifth and final card is dealt. It too will be face-up. We're on **fifth street**. All players who have not folded now hold one hole card and four open cards. There is a final round of betting at the upper tier of bets and then, if two or more players remain, the **showdown**, with the highest ranking poker hand claiming the pot.

As in all poker variations, a player can win the pot anytime before the showdown by forcing out all opponents through bets and raises that they won't match.

VARIOUS RULES

In five-card stud, the ace may be used as a high card or low card (to form a straight), though if there is an ace on board, it will count as a high card for the order of betting. There is a three-raise limit for each betting round, unless play goes heads-up, where players may raise back and forth as often as they like. Note, again, that completing the bring-in bet on the first betting round is not considered a raise.

8. OMAHA

Omaha high, which is also called **Omaha**, is a high poker game that is played exactly like hold'em, except for two things:

- Players get *four* cards to start with, as opposed to just two as in hold'em.

- Each player *must* use exactly two of his pocket cards, not more, not less, together with three from the board, to form his final five-card hand.

Omaha is played with a button, which moves clockwise around the table after each deal, as well as a small blind and a big blind. The deal starts with each player getting four downcards, called pocket cards or hole cards. The first betting round proceeds exactly as in hold'em, with the player to the left of the big blind acting first.

When the betting action has been completed on the preflop round, the flop of three community cards is turned face-up in the center of the table. This is followed by a round of betting. The turn and river cards are similarly dealt, each followed by a betting round. At the showdown, the highest hand wins the pot.

In limit games, all bets in the first round are in the lower increment: $3 in a $3/$6 game, $5 in a $5/$10 game, $15 in a $15/$30 game, and so on. If you were playing pot-limit, then you could bet up to the amount in the pot, and if no-limit were being played, your maximum bet would be limited only by the amount of chips you had on the table. Betting on the turn and the river must be at the higher level of the betting structure. For example, $6 in a $3/$6 game, $10 in a $5/$10 game, and $30 in a $15/$30 game.

It is easy to misread your hand in Omaha. For example, if

you were dealt four aces in the hole, you wouldn't have quads because only two of the aces would count toward the final hand! The remaining three cards would have to come from the board.

Omaha can also be played as high-low in a variation called **Omaha high-low 8-or-better** or simply, **Omaha 8-or-better**. In this version, the best low hand and best high hand split the pot. However, if no hand qualifies for low—has five unpaired cards of 8 or lower—the best high hand scoops (wins the entire pot). Players can choose two different five-card combinations to make their final hands, one for the high hand and one for the low hand.

The best high hand and best low hand can be held by the same player; if so, that player also scoops.

HOW TO READ AN OMAHA HIGH-LOW HAND

Here is an example showing how a high and low hand is made in conjunction with the board. If you hold A-A-J-4 with a board of A-J-7-6-2, two aces from your pocket cards are used to form the high hand, A-A-A-J-7.

The ace and 4 would be combined with the 7-6-2 of the board to form a 7-6-4-2-A for low.

Note that in both instances, two of your downcards and three community cards are used to make the final poker hand.

YOU HOLD

THE BOARD

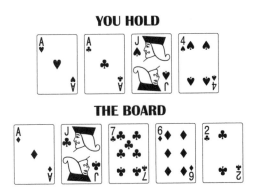

YOUR FINAL HIGH HAND

YOUR FINAL LOW HAND

Note that you don't have a full house of aces over jacks for the high hand because, again, you can only use two of your hole cards. If your opponent holds 3-3-3-J, he would lose on the high end since he only has a pair of jacks! Since he must use his jack as part of the hand, he does not have a 7-6-3-2-A low, so he would lose on the low end as well.

9. TOURNAMENT POKER

Tournaments are set up as a process of elimination. As players lose their chips and are eliminated from a tournament, the remaining competitors get consolidated into fewer tables. What might start out as a 200 player event played at twenty ten-handed tables will get reduced to nineteen tables, and then eighteen tables, and so on, as players bust out.

Eventually, the field will get narrowed down to just one table, the **final table**, where the prestige and big money is earned. And that table will play down until just one player is left holding all the chips—the **champion**.

REBUY AND FREEZE-OUT TOURNAMENTS

There are two types of tournaments—freeze-outs and rebuy tournaments. A **freeze-out tournament** is a do or die structure. Once you run out of chips, you are eliminated. Unlike a cash game, you can't go back into your pocket for more chips.

In a **rebuy tournament**, you can purchase additional chips, which is usually allowed only when your chip stack is equal to or less than the original starting amount and only during the first few specified rounds of play. This is called the **rebuy period**. Some tournaments allow limited rebuys, and others allow players to rebuy as often as they go broke, that is, until the rebuy period is over.

At the end of the rebuy period, most tournaments allow you to get an **add-on** as well—a final purchase of a specific amount of additional chips. Usually, only one add-on is permitted per player, though some events allow double add-ons, and rarely, even more.

Once the rebuy period is over, you're playing in pure

survival mode. If you lose your chips, you are eliminated and your tournament is over.

INSIDER TIP

FREEROLL TOURNAMENTS
To maintain the interest of their customers, attract new ones, and as a bonus to existing players, online sites run **freeroll tournaments**, tournaments where players can enter for free while qualifying for prize money or free entry into larger buy-in tournaments with big prizes. These tournaments are great because you get to play at no cost and get lots of practice. Should you get to the top of the ladder in an event giving away tournament entries, you can parlay an investment of nothing into something substantial.

SATELLITES AND SUPERSATELLITES

A **satellite** is a one-, sometimes two- or three-table tournament in which the winner gains entry into a larger buy-in tournament for a fraction of the cost. An online satellite gives you a great opportunity to parlay a small entry fee into a big payday. That's what Chris Moneymaker did in 2003 when he turned $40 online into $2.5 million and a championship title.

Supersatellites are multi-table tournaments with the same concept as satellites—for a low buy-in, players compete for a chance to win their way into a big buy-in event—except there are multiple winners in these larger tournaments.

SIT-AND-GOS

An increasingly popular online tournament is the sit-and-go, which is essentially a one-table tournament (though sit-and-gos could be two- or three-table tournaments as well). Players sign up for a sit-and-go at a buy-in they're comfortable with, and as soon as the table is filled, the cards are dealt and the tournament is on. Three places are paid in sit-and-gos. The winner is the last player remaining, and gets 50 percent of the buy-ins; the second place winner gets 30 percent, and the third place winner gets 20 percent.

There are three major attractions of online sit-and-go tournaments. First, most sit-and-gos are set up to take just one hour. Unlike bigger tournaments, which can take many hours, or, if they're big enough, many days, the sit-and-gos allow you to get in and out quickly. Fast blind increases insure that play moves rapidly. The second major attraction is that they can be profitable if you learn how to adjust your strategies for this particular poker form. And the third big benefit is that they give you a tremendous amount of practice for playing short-handed and heads-up poker.

As the table whittles down to just two players, you experience all the various dynamics of ten-player action to two-player action, which is especially valuable if you get to bigger tournaments and make a final table.

You can find sit-and-gos for a variety of entries, from ones with buy-ins for less than a $1 to events with buy-ins over $100. Sit-and-gos are usually listed online showing the buy-in and the rake (which is usually 10 percent of the buy-in), thus you'll see $5/50¢, $30/$3 and $50/$5, the second figure after the slash denoting the rake. The above buy-in and rake amounts can also be expressed as $5 + 50¢, $30 + $3 and $50 + $5, depending on the format the site likes to use.

The most popular sit-and-gos tend to be the $5/50¢, $10/$1, and $20/$2. At these limits, tables fill up fast. The higher level SNGs like $50/$5 and $100/$10 are less popular and may not fill up as quickly.

COSTS OF ENTERING

Entry fees for almost all online tournaments range from nothing (freerolls) to multi-table events with buy-ins of hundreds of dollars. It is rare to find online tournaments with buy-ins greater than $500, though now and again there are $1,000 buy-in tournaments, and rarely, ones for $10,000 or higher.

TOURNAMENT STRUCTURE

Tournaments are divided into **levels** or **rounds**. Each level is marked by an increase in the amount of chips players are forced to commit to the pot before the cards are dealt. The blinds slowly increase, and after a few levels, the antes kick in. The typical online tournament increases its levels every 10 to 15 minutes, with the higher buy-in events having the longer levels.

In big online tournaments that will last many hours, players might be given ten-minute breaks every sixty minutes, or fifteen minutes every two hours. Dinner breaks, which are standard in live tournaments, are not usually done online.

STARTING CHIP COUNTS

Your starting chip total in tournaments is determined in advance. In low-limit events, a $30 buy-in might give you $500 in chips, though you could just as easily be given you $30, $200 or $1,000. There is not necessarily any correlation between buy-in amounts and the number of chips you receive, though online, multi-table tournaments tend to give players $1,000, $1,500, $2,000 or $3,000 in starting chips, and sit-and-gos, $1,500.

However, whether you are given $1,000, $1,500, $3,000 or $10,000 in chips, you are on a level playing field with your competitors. In a tournament, everyone starts with the same number of chips. It will then be up to your skill and your luck to see how far you make it into the tournament.

TOURNAMENT PRIZE POOL

Most tournaments are set up so that approximately 10 percent to 15 percent of all players (and sometimes as high as 20 percent) will win cash prizes. The number of paid places, those who finish **in the money**, is usually posted soon after the tournament begins, as the poker site software calculates the total number of entrants and figures out how many places will be paid and the amount that will be paid to each winner.

TOURNAMENT DISCONNECTS

If you get disconnected in a tournament, hands will continue to be dealt and the event will proceed, even if the interruption is beyond your control. If the disconnect occurs during the play of a hand, you will be given a short period of time, perhaps thirty seconds to reconnect. If you are unable to do so, your hand will be considered folded (unless you have already moved all-in, in which case, the hand will be played to the end). Once you have been folded due to a disconnection, you will remain out of play, and your blinds will be collected, until you check the appropriate box to rejoin the game.

TOURNAMENT BLINDS AND ANTES

Unlike cash games, there is no manual posting of blinds or antes in the tournaments. They will be automatically collected at the appropriate times.

SECTION III
Online Basics

I. GETTING SET UP

To play online, you must have a Windows-based computer and access to the Internet, preferably high-speed access like DSL or cable. (Most sites cannot be accessed through an Apple.) If you've purchased a computer in the last several years, you'll have no problem meeting the minimum system requirements of any online poker site, so that shouldn't be a concern of yours. In any case, the download page will list the system requirements.

FIVE STEPS FOR GETTING SET UP

1. Choose a Site

First, you have to pick an online poker room where you want to play, and go to its website.

2. Download the Software

On the opening screen of the online poker site will be a prominent "Download" or "Download Now" button. Click on this button to download the poker room's software onto your computer. You may have several prompts to click during this process. Just follow along with the instructions on your screen. When the software has completed downloading, the poker site's icon will appear on your desktop.

The Download Button

3. Launch the Program

Double-click on the poker room's icon and you will automatically be taken to the site's home page.

4. Set Up Your Account

Before you can play—whether it's for free play or for real money—you'll need to officially register with the site. From the home page, click on the "Create Account," "Register Here" or similarly worded button. This will take you to the registration screen.

At the registration screen, you'll fill out your basic information—name, address, age and e-mail—and set up your unique user name and password. The online poker rooms, just like land-based casinos, want to make sure you're of legal age, which would be eighteen in most jurisdictions where they are based.

You'll also create a unique online identity, called a **screen name**, **alias** or **nickname**, which is the name you'll be represented with online. For example, you may call yourself "Poker2Joker," "GoToJoe," or maybe "GRichardG." No one else will have this identity online at the poker network. So if a name you like is already taken, you'll have to pick another until you have your own unique identity. (Be sure to choose your user name with appropriate language or it may be disallowed.)

When your information is complete, there will be a box to click "Yes" or "Enter," indicating that you have read the terms and conditions of the site. Once this is accomplished, you will be signed up and officially ready to go. Now you can play anytime by double-clicking the site's logo on your desktop. Type your username and password to log on, click "Okay" or "Enter," and you're ready to play.

5. Play for Money or Play for Free

If you're playing for free, you're ready to join the games. The site will provide you with funny money (chips that have no cash value). But if you want to play for real money, you'll need to get funds into your account to start playing. Let's see what this is about.

2. DEALING WITH MONEY ONLINE

In the lobby of your poker room will be a button marked something like "Cashier" or "My Account," which you can click on to check your account information, or make deposits and withdrawals. In that same section, will be information that explains their policies and procedures for financial transactions. Since real money is at stake, you may want to familiarize yourself with the particulars.

This section will go over some basics for depositing and withdrawing money to your online poker room account, plus some basics of your account screen. Let's start with deposits.

DEPOSITING MONEY INTO YOUR ACCOUNT

If you want to play for real money, you'll need to have funds deposited into your online poker room account. There are many options to achieve this, from using your credit card to depositing money in the old-fashioned way, by check. While all sites will accept credit cards as a means of depositing money into your account (which is the easiest way to deposit funds) not all credit cards will allow this type of transaction, especially in countries like the United States that frown upon online gambling.

The good news is that your online site will be right up to date on the best ways to get money in and out of your account, so it will always be easy to know all the options for getting your account funded. Below are the commonly accepted options for funding your online poker account starting with the two most popular methods: credit and debit cards and online e-wallets.

Credit and Debit Cards

In many countries around the world (though not the United States), you can deposit money directly into your online account using a credit card such as Visa or Mastercard, or debit cards put out by these companies and others. The vast bulk of online deposits into players' accounts are achieved through these methods.

Some banks may not allow transfers from your credit or debit cards to a gaming site (this applies to U.S. customers), and other banks may restrict the amount that is made available; but again, your online site will have the latest information on the best options.

Online E-Wallet

The second most popular method for players to deposit money online is through online e-wallet solutions such as NETeller and Moneybookers. E-wallets are accepted by all the sites and allow you almost instant access to your funds—that is, once your account is set up. This will usually take a few minutes in most cases, though it could be several days if there are complications. But once this is established, you can easily move funds back and forth between your e-wallet account and your online site.

After you sign up with an e-wallet company, you can use your credit or debit cards to deposit money into that account or make a transfer from your bank, and from there, you can get the funds over to your Internet poker account. You can also link up your bank account and set up EFT (Electronic Fund Transfers) for quick transfers of money into your e-wallet account. Note that e-wallets are not just useful for getting money into your poker-playing account; they can be used for all sorts of online purchases and money transfers.

Online poker rooms have prominent links to the e-wallet companies that are best for their customers so you'll have no problems figuring out your best options. Typically, these options are posted right on the home page itself, but if not, they are readily accessible in the same section where deposit information is explained. If you're unclear with the procedures or have questions and need help, you can always contact the site's customer support team. This department will be well versed on all the deposit and withdrawal methods available.

Getting Credits From a Friend

Most sites allow you to transfer funds to other players on the same site. If you have a friend who plays on the same site as you do, and need to get money, you can transfer funds from his account into yours, and back again, as desired.

Wire Transfer

Wire transfers are an easy way to get money into your account. This is not the most popular method of depositing, as most players prefer using plastic or e-wallets, but it is an option. Check with your local bank for information on how to arrange wire transfers into your online account. The downside of wire transfers is that your bank will sometimes charge a higher fee for the service, but you can always check with it to find out. In most cases, expect a wire transfer to take anywhere from one day to three days.

Personal Check

Using personal checks is your least desirable option because after your check is received, you must wait for your money to clear before it can be posted to your account. In other words, it will be *slow*. If you're impatient, you will have a long, frustrating wait before you can begin playing. For obvious reasons, players rarely deposit by check.

Money Order/Bank Check

You may also mail deposits by money orders or bank checks, but again, like personal checks, it is not a desirable option. You still have the time delay until your funds get to the site, then perhaps some days for these checks to clear. For the same effort, you can go into a bank and make a wire transfer, which would get money into your account quickly and safely. If you'll be mailing a check, it is recommended that you send it by a delivery method where a signature is required.

INSIDER TIP

DEPOSITING IN VARIOUS CURRENCIES
You should be able to deposit money in any of the major currencies, such as euros (€), pounds (£), Swedish Krona (SEK) and U.S. dollars ($), and many, if not all, of the minor currencies as well. Check with the site if you have any questions.

Prepaid Cards

A newer form of getting money into your account is by prepaid ATM-type cards, such as Paysafe, where you use cash to buy an equivalent money value of credits onto your card, and then use the card to deposit into your account. Again, check with your poker room's deposit page or customer support to see if they have a relationship with prepaid cards that will work for you.

WITHDRAWING MONEY FROM YOUR ACCOUNT

Okay, you've won money with some great play and now want to withdraw the loot from your account and do something else with it. What do you do?

Each site will provide you with instructions on how to withdraw your money, but if you're unclear, you can always get assistance from customer support.

The most popular methods of withdrawal are wire transfers made by the online poker site directly to your bank account, checks sent through the mail, or money credited back to your credit or debit card or into your e-wallet account. Withdrawal requests are typically processed within twenty-four hours, the delay being due to a manual verification process online sites use to protect against fraud. The actual amount of time it will

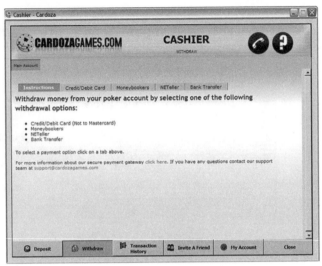

Withdrawal Screen A

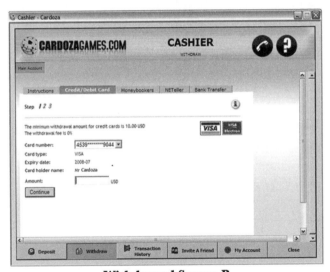

Withdrawal Screen B

take for you to receive your funds from the time the transaction is approved will vary from instantaneous (e-wallets and credit cards) to a week or two (checks mailed to foreign destinations), depending on the method chosen for withdrawal.

Given the various ways that sites handle withdrawals, it is recommended that you check the withdrawals page of your poker room for the terms and conditions so you fully understand the policies and procedures established by your poker room.

E-Wallet

If you have an e-wallet account set up, it's easy to move funds out of your online playing account back to your e-wallet (and vice-versa). This is the preferred method for serious online poker pros that like to play at various sites and use their e-wallet as a central base to fund their various online accounts.

Wire Transfer

Sites will usually wire money back into your account if you click this option for making your withdrawal, especially if this is how you got money into your account in the first place. The transfer could take as little as one day or as long as three to five days, depending on the time of the transfer, how the banks communicate with one another, and the day of week that the process is started (you'll have delays if the transfer is done on days the bank is closed, such as weekends and holidays).

Credit and Debit Cards

Some credit cards allow players to get their buy-ins or winnings deposited back onto their credit or debit cards (for example, Visa offers this service as of this writing), while others will not allow it at all (for example, Mastercard, as of this writing). There is typically a small fee for this process, however, as a service for their customers, most Internet poker rooms will absorb that amount (for example, cardozagames.com pays all fees of this nature for its customers) so that players get the full value of their withdrawal.

Company Check

If the above routes are not chosen, the poker room can make out a bank check or money order and mail it to the address listed on your account. This may take a week or so, depending on the speed of the site and the mail, so don't depend on this payment method if you're in dire need of immediately paying a bill with that money.

Giving Credits to a Friend

If you get them from a friend, you can give them as well, and settle up the funds separately.

CHECKING YOUR ACCOUNT STATUS

There are options on all sites that allow you to view your account balance and transaction history, manage deposits and withdrawals, and view the current amount that is still in your account. It may be called "Cashier" or "My Account." Generally, all your previous financial transactions—including deposits, cashouts and bonuses—are accessible from this account screen.

When you leave a cash game, your final chip total will go back into your account, waiting until you make it available for playing in another game or choose to withdraw some or all of it. So if you had $500 in your account, withdrew $100 as a buy-in for a cash game, bringing your account down to $400, and after, cashed out with $180 (the $80 representing your winnings), your new account balance would show $580.

Similarly, if you pulled $100 out of your $500 bankroll to enter a tournament and won $2,500 (including your $100 buy-in), your new account balance would be $2,900.

3. GETTING INTO GAMES

If the world of Internet poker is a new experience for you, you're in for a nice surprise: Playing online is easy. You'll see. In just minutes, you'll feel like an old hand at the virtual tables. However, before you join a real-money game, you should take a few minutes to get familiar with the site's interface and the various options available.

If you've already played online poker but are trying out a new site, you'll find the basics of play and the options similar from one site to another. And even though you can jump right in and play, you may consider spending a few minutes checking out the software and perhaps take advantage of the free-money games before you get into the cash games. Forget about the bad play you'll encounter at these tables. The point is to get familiar with the poker-playing interface.

In the lobby of your poker room, you'll find menus displaying all the games in progress and the basic information about each one of them. The list will be broken down by types of games available, number of players, average pot size, whether a multi-table tournament, sit-and-go, or a cash game is being played, and so on—in other words, all the information you need about whether a game is right for you.

You'll have a wide variety of choices. If it's cash games you want to play, you can choose from limit, pot-limit, and no-limit variations at a wide variety of stakes, even as low as penny-ante games. There will be hold'em games, Omaha and seven-card stud. You may also find less-popular games like five-card stud or draw-poker variations. If you prefer tournaments, there is everything from one and two table sit-and-gos, to massive tournaments where anywhere from a few dozen to thousands

of players compete for cash prizes or coveted seats to the World
Series of Poker and other major events. And if you want to test
the games before playing or just want to have fun without risking
your money, free-money tables are readily available.

For each of the types of games, there are menus that display
your choices and whether or not seats are available for you to
join the game.

THE POKER LOBBY

Okay, you've registered with your site, deposited funds (or
will be playing for free), and are aching to get going. Once you
have the software installed on your computer and double-clicked
on the site's icon, it will go to the homepage where you'll log on.
The software will ask you for your screen name and password.
Click the "Enter" or "Okay" button.

You'll be in the poker lobby, the nexus of the poker room,
where you can do everything you need to do.

HOW TO CHOOSE A GAME

All your poker-playing choices are displayed front and center
in the lobby. This screenshot below, from cardozagames.com,
shows how your game choices might be displayed online.

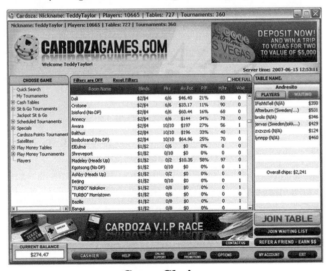

Game Choices

In the left-hand column, you see an area marked "Choose Game" with headings for Quick Search, My Tournaments, Cash Tables, Sit & Go Tournaments, Scheduled Tournaments, Specials, Play Money Tables, Play Money Tournaments, and a few other choices. To the left of some of these headings is a plus "+" sign. The "+" indicates that you have more choices available by clicking on that symbol.

INSIDER TIP

"+" AND "-" SYMBOLS

Whenever you see a "+" symbol, it indicates that there are further subsets you can access by clicking on it. And when you see a "-" symbol, clicking on it will condense the subsets so you see only the header, keeping your choices more organized.

In the following screen, you see a further breakdown of no-limit hold'em games under the Choose Game section, ranging from $100/$200 NL, a pretty big cash game, down to $0.10/$0.20 and <$0.10 NL, microlimit games played for pennies.

When you click on this "+" symbol, a drop down menu appears showing the various poker variations offered, plus a few specialty tables like Beginners' Tables and Heads Up (explained later). We've decided to play no-limit hold'em, so we've clicked on that "+" symbol (so it now displays a "-" symbol). Of course, if you prefer other games, like Omaha or seven-card stud, you would click on those options.

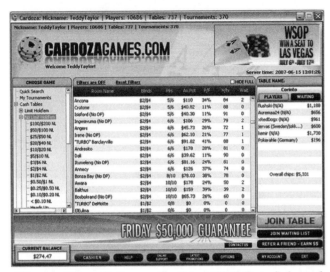

Choose Game Column: No-Limit Hold'em Selected

In this next screen, we clicked on the $1/$2 headers to see what's available at those stakes. You see that "$1/$2 NL" is highlighted under No-Limit Hold'em in the Choose Game section on the left, while on the right side, in the big display area, is a listing of $1/$2 no-limit hold'em games.

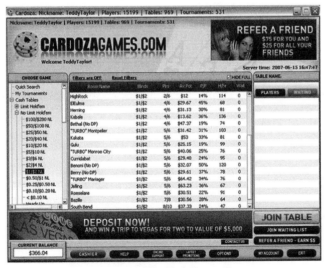

$1/$2 No-Limit Hold'em Games

Search Feature

Your poker room allows you to find games that exactly fit the criteria you're looking for. The screenshot below from cardozagames.com shows you what a poker room's search feature might look like.

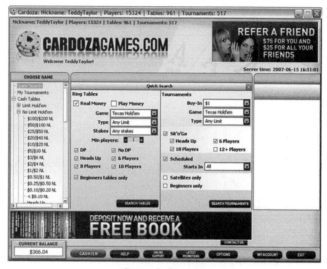

Search Screen

┌───┐
│ **INSIDER TIP** │ ### EACH POKER NETWORK USES A DIFFERENT INTERFACE

Each poker network will organize their poker lobbies differently. For example, you may find the poker variations organized by tabs at the top, as opposed to the listings on the side. But whatever the layout, it will be pretty clear how to find the games you want to play.

How to Choose a Cash Game

The beauty of online play is that you can use the information provided in the lobby screen to choose the table that best suits your style and preferences before you put your money in action! The information about each game will be clearly displayed so you can make better decisions on the best game for you. I've used headings from cardozagames.com to illustrate how this particular poker room organizes its poker lobby.

Room Name, Table or **Game**: Indicates the assigned name for this table. Special conditions may be stated in parenthesis.

Blinds: Displays the small blind and the big blind.

Plrs or **Players** or **Seated**: This column shows the number of players the table holds and how many are currently playing. The first number represents the number of occupied seats and the second, after the slash (/), the seating capacity of the table. A listing of 6/10 indicates that six players are seated at a ten-player table (four seats available) and 8/8 shows that an eight-player table is full.

Avg. Pot: Displays the average pot size at this table averaged over "X" number of previous hands.

P/F or **Plrs/flop**: Displays the percentage of players, averaged over "X" number of previous hands, who were dealt cards and stayed in to see the flop.

H/Hr or **Hnds/Hr**: Displays the number of dealt hands per hour. This allows you to see how fast or slow the game is moving.

Wait: The number of players on a waiting list, if any. Here is another heading you may find for hold'em or Omaha.

Stakes: In limit games, displays the two-tier betting structure, such as $5/$10, and in no-limit or pot-limit, may simply display the blind amounts.

In the stud games, there are no blinds so instead of a column for Blinds and P/F or Plrs/flop, you'll see information for the stakes of the game and percentage of players who reach fourth street. For example, you might see these headers for the columns:

SORTING TIP

By clicking on the headers for the individual columns, you can usually sort the information by that column. For example, if you click on the Av.Pot, it will list the pot sizes from smallest at the top to largest on the bottom. Click again, and it will reverse sort, showing average pot sizes with the largest on the top and the smallest on the bottom. The same top-to-bottom and bottom-to-top sorting applies to the other columns as well.

Stakes: Five- and seven-card stud are almost always played as limit games, so the two-tier betting structure shown here indicates the size of the game.

Plrs/4th: The average number of players who see their fourth card.

Antes: The ante required for each hand.

HOW TO CHOOSE A TOURNAMENT

With the exception of sit-and-gos, which will begin as soon as a table fills up with players, tournaments are scheduled for specific days and times. Sites will sometimes run their own private tournaments, open only to their members, though usually, the tournaments are organized on a network-wide basis. Bigger online tournaments, ones that generate a lot of excitement, will often be advertised on the poker room's home page.

You'll find all the tournament listings in the area marked "Tournaments" or "Tourney." The schedule of listed events here will show the buy-in amount, starting times, type of tournament, and other relevant information.

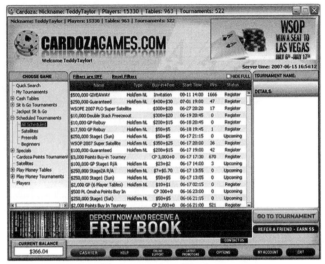

Tournament Choices

Here are some column headings you may see for tournaments:

Name: Displays the name of the tournament and some additional information.

Type: The poker variation being played, for example, NLHE (no-limit hold'em), PLO (pot-limit Omaha), or simply NL (no-limit).

Buy-In + Fee: The entry fee to play plus the house rake.

Start Time: When the tournament begins.

Plrs: The number of players already entered into the event.

Status: The information in this column will let you know whether you can still sign up ("Register"), or that the tournament is ongoing and it is too late to sign up ("In progress"), or that it is completed ("Finished").

SPECIALIZED ONLINE GAMES

Over time, several types of online games have evolved in response to players who wanted better choices. Besides the classifications of games being Real Money or Play Money, Cash or Tournament (and Sit-and-Go), there are four options you'll see online that could apply to any of these game types. These are shown below.

Some Specialized Game Options

Beginner Tables

The Beginner Tables allow new players to compete against other new players while they get adjusted to the site. Upon registering, a player is eligible to compete at designated beginner tables for a limited period of time, usually three months, after which time, the site assumes the player is no longer a beginner and then disallows him from further play at these tables.

Turbo or Fast Games

If you like to play fast poker, you can join games that are noted as "**Turbo**." This speed setting typically gives players only fifteen seconds before they have to make their decision—or they will get timed out. Auto-posting of blinds and antes are required at turbo tables. Turbo also applies to sit-and-go tournaments with fast levels.

Super Turbo Sit-and-gos and Tournaments

The **Super Turbo** sit-and-gos and tournaments have extremely fast rounds, some as quick as three minutes per level, or even one minute per level, and others where the blind goes up after every hand. Very fast decision-making is also required on each hand.

No DP Tables or No All-In

"No DP" stands for "No Disconnect Policy." Games marked with the "No DP" or "No All-In" distinction, typically in parenthesis after the table name, don't have the normal disconnect protections on a site. In instances in which a player loses his connection at a No DP or No All-In table, he gets extra time to reconnect. However, if contact is not made, his hand automatically gets folded.

HOW TO JOIN A GAME

To join a game, double-click on your desired table from the list, or alternatively, highlight the game you like and click the "Join Table," "Go to Table," or similarly worded button. These actions will open up the poker table on your screen and display the game in progress.

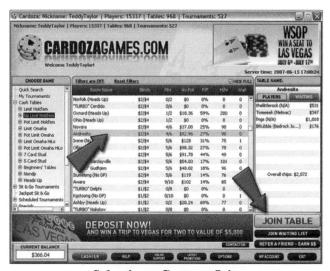

Selecting a Game to Join

Available seats will either be marked by wording such as "Seat Open" or they will be visibly empty (no avatars or names listed by the chair)—or both. You select your seat by clicking directly on it. That will prompt the software to display the buy-in screen.

To Join the Game, Click on the Seat You Want

Waiting List

If you want to enter a particular game that's already full, you put your name on the waiting list by clicking on a table and selecting the button marked with language like "Join Waiting List." Then you enter the appropriate information or click the appropriate boxes to get in the queue.

When a seat becomes available and it's your turn in the queue, a popup screen will appear, with language like, "A seat is reserved for you at X table (Texas Hold'em $2/$4, 8 players.) You have X seconds to claim it. Would you like to take the seat?" You will also be notified by a beeping noise. (If you're not right at your computer, keep its volume high enough so that you can hear the alert.)

If you still wish to join the table, click the "Yes" or "OK" prompt. If you decide you no longer wish to play, simply select "No," or just ignore the prompt. If you click "Yes" or "OK," the table will open up on your screen and you will be asked to buy-in.

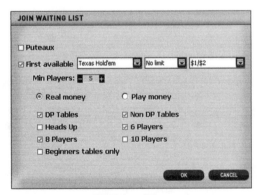

Waiting List

BUYING IN

When you click to join a cash game, a popup screen will appear with something like this: "How much money would you like to bring to the table?" This screen will also display how much you currently have available in your bankroll and the minimum and maximum buy-in for the game. On this screen, you'll choose the amount of your buy-in.

Your buy-in must always be within the minimum and maximum limits set for the game; the software will not allow you to enter a game with any amounts outside of these limits. Additional buy-ins, should you need them later, must also be within the minimum and maximum stated limits.

Enter your buy-in, click "OK" or "Yes," and your screen name and table bankroll will appear by the seat you have chosen.

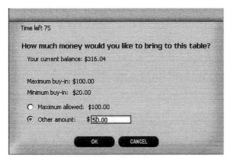

Buy-In Screen

Your buy-in amount will be taken from the total bankroll amount that you have available with the poker site. (Obviously, you'll have to have funds in your account to make the buy-in.) Funds that you do not use for your buy-in will remain in your account. For example, if you have $500 in your account and choose $100 as a buy-in, the $100 would appear as your stakes for the game chosen with the other $400 remaining safely in your account. It's like pulling out $100 from your wallet, putting in on the table in a cash game, and putting the rest away in your pocket—only the $100 can be accessed during a hand.

During play, your table bankroll will increase and decrease according to your wins or losses. When you exit a game and return to the lobby, the remaining balance from your game will be added to your total bankroll. Continuing our prior example, if you exit the table with $175, your account will show a total of $575—the $400 that remained in your account plus the added $175 from this table.

Should your table funds be less than the big blind at the completion of any hand, you will need to purchase more chips to continue playing, subject to the limits stated for the game. A screen will automatically pop up, asking if you want to buy in for more chips or to exit the game.

Some sites will post the buy-in in its own column on the lobby page. If there is only one number shown, this amount will always represent the maximum buy-in. For example, you might see $200 listed in the BUY-IN column for a no-limit or pot-limit game. This tells you the *maximum* allowed buy-in for the table. The minimum buy-in is usually 10–20 percent of the maximum (it varies by the site), so in the example above, it might be anywhere from $20 to $40. (In limit games, the minimum buy-in is often ten or twenty times the lower limit bet, so that in a $5/$10 game, it might be $50 or $100.)

	WATCH BEFORE YOU PLAY!
INSIDER TIP	Online sites allow you to watch games in progress without actually participating in them. Use this feature to check out a game before deciding whether or not to join.

OBSERVING GAMES

If you just want to watch a game as a railbird, its simple to do. Just open the table (as above) and don't do anything! You'll see the cards just like any participant in the game, except that, obviously, you won't be able to view any players' hole cards. If you decide to join the game later and a seat is available, you can hop in there as you normally would—by clicking on an empty seat—or, if the table is full, you can put your name on the waiting list. Some players like to railbird top players to learn from their moves or just to see how a game proceeds, especially one they may wish to play in.

GETTING READY TO PLAY

Okay, you've made a buy-in, and your avatar and table bankroll (buy-in) will appear at a seat. The procedures for joining a game in progress vary depending upon whether you are playing a game with blinds, or one that has antes. Let's look at both.

Joining Hold'em and Omaha (Blind Games)

In online hold'em and Omaha games, you cannot enter play until you've posted a big blind bet. After you've made your buy-in, you may be alerted by a screen that says something like "Wait for Big Blind?" You can choose to do this, waiting until the blind naturally reaches your position. Or, you can choose to immediately enter the game.

If you choose to join the game immediately, without waiting for the big blind to reach your seat, you will have to post an additional big blind to the one already being posted in the big blind position. Now, there will be two big blinds and a small blind. If two new players had entered at the same time without waiting for the big blind to come to them, there would be three big blinds and one small blind. Theoretically, you could have eight big blinds in a ten-player game (you cannot enter a game from the small blind or the button positions).

Option to Post Big Blind Early

AUTO-POST BLIND

Upon joining a table, or after you see the blinds for the first time, a popup screen may appear giving you the option to auto-post the blind. You can also click on the Auto Post Blind button. Choosing this convenient feature automatically places your blind bets when due and prevents the game from being held up unnecessarily. Some players don't choose this option, much to the chagrin of opponents who get stuck waiting for their opponents' blinds to be manually posted before the cards can be dealt.

Joining Five- and Seven-Card Stud (Ante Games)

In games where antes are required, such as five- and seven-card stud, you have the option to have your antes automatically placed before each deal by clicking on the Auto Ante or a similarly worded button. This useful feature speeds up the game on tables where the ante is not automatically posted by the software. You may get a prompt such as "To speed up play, would you like to use the auto-ante feature?" I would recommend choosing this option.

START PLAYING!

You've got chips, you've got a seat, and you've got a game. Go get 'em cowboy!

4. HOW TO PLAY POKER ONLINE

Though different sites might use different graphics, and offer slightly different game-playing options, you'll find that poker is poker. The betting choices on one site will be pretty much the same as on another. The user interface—how you interact with the game—will have different looks and feels, but in the end, they all do the same thing—allow you to play poker.

HOW TO BET, RAISE, CALL AND CHECK

When it's your turn to play, audio and visual prompts will let you know that you have to act. Your betting options for the round will automatically be displayed below the poker layout. If there is a bet on the table when it is your turn to play, you'll see options for "Fold," "Call," and "Raise." If no bet is due, you'll have options for "Fold," "Check," or "Bet" instead.

Additionally, the software will display how much the call needs to be and how much a raise can be. Thus, if a player opens for $2, the buttons may show "Fold," "Call $2," and "Raise $4," or if no bet is due, then the bet button may say "Bet $2" if it's a $2/$4 game. Of course, while folding is an option if no bets have yet been made, it would be foolish to do so when you might get to see another card without risk if your opponents check as well.

Following are two screen shots showing your betting options on the flop; one before a bet is made, another after a bet is made.

Your Options: No Bet Yet Made

Your Options: A $2 Bet Has Been Made

BETS ARE FINAL

Remember that once you click on an action button, your bet is final—it cannot be taken back, even if you had unintentionally clicked on the wrong button. This is just like live poker played anywhere. A bet is *always* a bet. So, before clicking, be careful that your betting actions are what you want them to be.

PRE-SELECT OR EARLY ACTION BETTING OPTIONS

The pre-select or early action betting options are one of the great features of online poker that are not available in live games. During the play of a hand, a set of options will appear allowing you to choose a play in *advance* of your turn. This greatly speeds up the game, and allows you to temporarily turn your attention elsewhere while the round plays out.

For example, if you're dealt 10-6 and know that you're going to fold, you can pre-select the Fold option and when play comes around to your position, your hand will be automatically folded.

Your pre-selected action is not immediately revealed to your opponents—only you know what your action will be—so opponents won't know what decision you've made until it is your turn to act and that play is revealed. But on the other hand, the quickness of the action will let them know, *after* the fact, that you had probably chosen an early action button to make that play. There is a disadvantage to that, which we'll take a closer look at in the Specific Online Strategies chapter.

The early action buttons commonly used are Fold, Check/ Fold, Call, Call Any, Raise, Raise Any, and Bet Pot. They will only be displayed in situations where they are appropriate. Also, if the option you chose is no longer valid by the time play gets to your position, the pre-select will be cancelled and your regular play options will be displayed. For example, if you pre-select a $5 call but the pot has been raised to $10, your $5 call obviously won't be valid and you will be shown a new set of available choices.

The following screenshots show some pre-selects you might see in a limit hold'em game.

Preflop Early Action Betting Options

Postflop Early Action Betting Options

Let's look at how these particular pre-select options work:

COMMON PRE-SELECT OPTIONS

Fold: Checking the Fold option will cause your hand to be folded as soon as play reaches your position.

Check/Fold: Clicking on the Check/Fold button allows you to stay active in a hand if no one bets, but fold, if someone does.

Call: This allows you to call the current bet in advance of your turn. But if the pot gets raised, your call decision is nullified and new options will appear.

Call Any: This limit poker option allows you to automatically meet any bets (or raises) that are made.

Raise or **Raise Min**: In limit poker, this pre-select will initiate a standard raise when the action reaches the bettor. In no-limit, the raise button usually pre-selects the minimum amount that can be raised. In either case, if the pot gets raised above the current level, the pre-select option will no longer be valid.

Raise Any: This limit poker option automatically raises any bet or raise when it's your turn to act.

Bet Pot: In pot-limit and no-limit, a pre-select that allows you to match what is in the pot with a bet or raise.

BETTING DISPLAYS

In online poker, it's always easy to see who's made bets, or folded, and where the action is. In fact, it's done the same way as in a live game. In a cardroom, a player's bet or raise will stay in front of his spot until all bets have been called. Only then does the dealer sweep all bets into the pot. Online, when a bet or raise is made, a representation of the chip amount wagered will be displayed in front of the bettor along with that actual amount with $ signs so that you can clearly see the total bet.

And if a player folds, just like a live game, his cards will be removed. So, for example, before any action has occurred on the preflop, you'll see the two blind bets displayed. Let's say the first two players fold, the following player calls, the next one raises to $20, and the following four players fold. Here is what the screen would look like in a no-limit hold'em game with blinds of $2.50/$5:

No-Limit Hold'em Game: Preflop Betting

You can see the active players (those with the chips in front of their positions), the folded players (those with their cards removed from play), and the betting choices available for the next player to act. The action is now on the little blind.

When all bets and raises have been completed during a betting round, the bets will no longer appear in front of each player, but will automatically be added to the amount of the pot, which will be displayed in the center of the table.

TIME LIMITS: REGULAR GAMES

Online sites give you a certain amount of time to act, usually twenty to thirty seconds. At that time if you haven't acted, you will be **timed-out**, and your hand will automatically be folded, regardless of the cards you hold. You will be alerted with a series of beeps when your time is running out, and additionally, a warning will appear on your screen.

Clock Shows Time Running Out

The time-out feature prevents any one player from holding up the game indefinitely.

If you get timed out, you will hold your seat at the table but will not get dealt more hands until you manually click a button to rejoin the game.

Occasionally, you may require extra time on difficult decisions or be momentarily sidetracked by "real-world" distractions. However, you should be considerate of your opponents and make every effort to make your decisions in a timely manner. If you continually push the time limit to the maximum, the other players at the table will get annoyed. Everyone is there to play, not watch and wait. If you keep stalling, your opponents won't want to play with you, unless of course, you're losing lots of money. In that case, they'll find a way to persevere.

You may find that use of the pre-select option boxes will help you play more efficiently.

INSIDER TIP

ONLINE TIP

Keep your sound on if you're occupied or distracted by other activities or your eyes are away from your screen. The sound prompts will alert you when it's your time to play.

INTERNET CONNECTION LOSS

If you are involved in the middle of a hand, and either you or one of your opponents loses the connection, the screen will display a message along the lines of: "Player X has lost the connection and is trying to reconnect." The action at the table will freeze and give the disconnected player time, around two minutes (the amount of time and procedure varies by site), to reestablish his connection and resume play.

If the player cannot reestablish his connection, it will trigger an immediate all-in type situation. All betting ceases and uncalled bets or raises will be returned to the players and no further bets will be made. The cards then get automatically played out to the river with the best active hand taking down the truncated pot. For example, let's say you're on the turn, and bet $10 into a $55 pot. Suddenly, an opponent loses his connection (or you lose yours). The program will return the $10 since it was not yet called, play out the river card, and award the $55 pot to the best hand.

Disconnects, while annoying, do occur. It is one of the realities of online poker. At the same time, there are players who abuse this feature. Penalties for those players might include loss of disconnect privileges, and in extreme cases, expulsion from the site.

COMMUNITY STANDARDS AND ETIQUETTE

The majority of players online are there to enjoy a friendly and pleasant playing environment. Of course, there are many pros as well—just like in the live games—hammering out a living. In both environments, there is an etiquette and code of conduct that should be respected so that the game is enjoyable for all.

Although individual sites cannot be held responsible for any player's conduct, if a player gets abusive or disrespectful, the poker room management might step in to warn the violator that this kind of behavior will not be tolerated. A serious breach of a site's rules may include the risk of suspension or a permanent ban.

For example, the following behaviors are serious breaches of etiquette—or worse.

Players may not:

- Use vulgar, offensive, racist, or obscene language

- Abuse, harass, bully or threaten other players or employees

- Reveal any cards held or passed or discuss any hand in progress

- Agree to check a hand down when a third player is all-in

- Needlessly slow down a game

- Make statements to induce a player to act in a certain way

- Communicate in any language other than English during a hand

- Collude with any other player, cheat, or illegally pass chips

CUSTOMER SUPPORT

Online poker sites are customer-oriented businesses that rely heavily on keeping their patrons satisfied. Part of that satisfaction process is prompt and helpful customer support. Of course, support issues will vary from site to site, and there may be glitches here and there, but overall, you'll find that the reputable sites take their customers' concerns seriously.

The online sites will have a help button and FAQ section to answer the most common questions. And if you don't find your answers there, contact customer support to get what you need. You'll find sites eager to attend to your concerns. Customer support teams are generally available 24/7—by telephone, email, and through online chat—to answer all your questions and concerns.

5. MORE ONLINE OPTIONS

There are many cool features available to you online and most of them are accessed through the lobby. You may see a button marked "Options," which will contain many of these possibilities. Let's see what a few of them are.

PLAYING MULTIPLE TABLES

You can play multiple tables *and* tournaments simultaneously and enjoy that many more times the action and fun. Some players will navigate back and forth between as many as eight or more games! At first, it might be tricky to pay attention to multiple games without getting confused, but soon enough, you'll get the hang of it. And if you're a player that likes a lot of action, this is how you'll get that action.

You open additional tables and buy in to those games just the way you opened your original one—from the lobby. You repeat this procedure for as many tables as you can handle, or the site can accommodate. The poker room will have a Mini-Table option, which reduces the screen size of each game, allowing you to view multiple tables simultaneously, and tile (layer) active screens for easy access between the games.

You can switch between tables by clicking on the table list on your screen, or, as most players do, by clicking on the tables themselves to activate that particular window and bring it to the front. Additionally, when it is your turn to play on one of the tables, the software on many sites will automatically bring that active screen to the front.

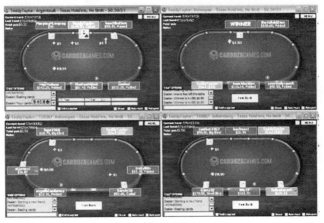

Four Tiled Tables

SITTING OUT

You have the option to temporarily sit out some hands during a game—perhaps to take a bathroom break or an important phone call—while holding your seat. You do this by clicking on the "Sit Out," "Deal Me Out," or similarly worded box. But you can't hold a seat forever. Sites limit how long you can occupy a seat without playing before they ask you to play or go away.

If the blind passes your spot three times (or whatever parameters are set by the poker room) and you still have not rejoined the game, you will be automatically removed from the table and your seat made available. If this occurs, don't worry, your chips will go right back into your bankroll!

HOW TO REJOIN A GAME

When you want to rejoin the game after sitting out, you either unclick the "Sit Out" button, or you may be presented with a button that says something like "I'm back," which you select to become active again. Or if you have been away too long and have been removed from the table, you can rejoin the game in the normal fashion.

If you miss a round in which you should have posted a blind and it has bypassed your position, then you have to post a "dead blind" (in effect, making two big blinds) to compensate for this. Sites do not allow players to go in and out of games to avoid the rotation of the blinds.

CHAT

The chat box allows you to communicate with your fellow players by typing in messages. For example, if a player wins a big pot, you can type in, "Good hand" or "Well played." Or, as experienced players do, "GH" or "WP." Internet poker has developed its own shorthand so that players can quickly and easily communicate with one another in the chat box.

In the glossary, there is list of acronyms that will be useful to you online, both for your own communication and so that your opponents' messages don't look like gibberish!

Usually, you can position the chat window anywhere you like by holding down your mouse button on the window, and moving it to another location on the screen. Of course, you don't want to put the chat window over the table itself, because it may cover up the cards or the bets!

AVATARS

An **avatar** is an on-screen icon that is used as your representation at the table. Each site provides their players with various options to choose from. They could be symbols, like flags or shapes, cartoon characters or animals, even an actual photo that you upload to the site. The avatar is what you and your opponents will see represented on the screen, your image, so to speak.

GAME ENVIRONMENT OPTIONS

Some online sites allow you to can customize certain elements of your game environment, such as the cards or background layouts. These changes are cosmetic only and do not affect how the game is played, or even how your opponents view the game—they are only available on your playing screen. If you get some free time when playing or are just kicking around, you can dig into your site's software to see the options available.

You'll also get some audio options to choose from. Your poker room's audio controls allow you to turn background sounds on or off and perhaps choose the level of ambient sounds that get played.

SHOW/MUCK

The show/muck option gives you a chance to show any hand that would not normally be revealed. At the conclusion of a hand in which you won, choose "Show" to reveal your cards to your opponents.

AUTO MUCK

The auto muck feature allows you to automatically toss your cards away during the showdown—just as in a regular poker game—if a prior player reveals a better hand than you.

FINDING PLAYERS ONLINE

You'll make lots of friends playing poker online! And you'll also find lots of players you like playing against. Online sites give you tools to locate friends and fellow players that are currently on their site so you can join in their games if seats are available, or just chat and see what they're up to. There are two features you may find, the Buddy List, which will display all the nicknames of players you have entered onto that list who are online and at what tables they are playing, and a search tool, which allows you to enter a player's nickname. If the search tool shows a player is online, it will also show the table he is playing at. You can use either of these tools to go directly to the table where your friends are playing and join the action.

INSIDER TIP

TRACKING THE FISH

A lot of players use the Buddy List to keep track of the fish (weak competition) when they are online, so they can play with them and pad their bankrolls.

Each site may handle these features differently, so you'll have to familiarize yourself with how it is done on your Internet poker site. Following are two examples from cardozagames.com so you can get a sense of what this might look like:

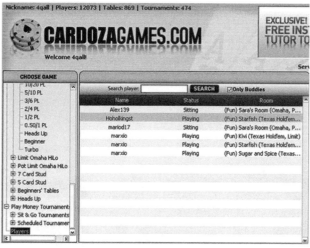

Buddy List

In the screenshot below, we've clicked on Begster, then selected the "Your buddy" checkbox. He is now on the Buddy List.

Adding Player to Buddy List

NOTEPAD

Another great feature online, which you don't have in live poker, is the use of a notepad where you can take notes on players' tendencies, weaknesses, strengths, or anything else you want to keep track of. These notes will remain in the site's memory and be accessible to you every time you log on. Unlike a live game, where it would be awkward to pull out a pad and make notes, no one knows you're jotting down things while you play online, nor would they care—it's all part of the online world.

If your site has this feature—and almost all of them do—make sure to take full advantage of it so when you encounter players in the future, you have a head start on what to expect and how best to play them.

Notepad

EARNING POINTS

Earn while you learn; earn while you play; and earn while you win. You can accumulate points, which are similar to frequent flier miles, while you play in cash games and tournaments online. Sites reward their good customers with points and that's good for you. Points may be used as buy-ins to online tournaments, exchanged for cash during promotional periods, or used to buy products, plane tickets, and even buy-ins for land-based poker tournaments around the world. Your poker room will have full descriptions of these benefits.

SECTION IV
Game Strategies

1. SEVEN RULES OF WINNING HOLD'EM

The following key concepts apply to all forms of hold'em.

1. RESPECT POSITION

In hold'em, where you sit relative to the button is called **position**. In a nine-handed game, the first three spots to the left of the button are known as **early position**, the next three, **middle position**, and the last three, **late position**. In a ten-handed game, early position is the four spots to the left of the button.

The later the position, the bigger the advantage, because you get to see what your opponents do before deciding whether to commit any chips to the pot. The earlier the position, the more vulnerable your hand is to being raised and thus the more powerful your hand must be for you to enter the pot.

In late position, you have more options and leverage so you can play more hands. If the early betting action is aggressive, you can fold marginal hands without cost. And if the betting action is weak, you can be more aggressive with marginal hands and see the flop with better position.

2. PLAY GOOD STARTING CARDS

You must start out with good cards to give yourself the best chance to win. And while this seems obvious, you'd be surprised at the number of players who ignore this basic strategic concept and take loss after loss by chasing inferior and losing hands. If you play too many hands in poker, you'll soon find yourself without chips. Enter the pot with good starting cards in the right position and you give yourself good chances to finish with winners.

3. PLAY OPPONENTS

By watching how an opponent plays, you get all sorts of information on how to take advantage of his tendencies. For example, when a player infrequently enters a pot, he's **tight**, and you can often force him out of hands even when he may have better cards than you. You'll give him credit for big hands when he's in a pot, and get out of his way unless you have a big hand yourself.

On the other hand, an opponent who plays a lot of hands is **loose**, and you can figure him for weaker cards on average. You also need to adjust for **aggressive** players, who often raise when they get involved in a pot, and **passive** players, opponents you can play against with less fear of getting raised.

4. BE THE AGGRESSOR

Hold'em is a game where aggression brings the best returns. It's almost always better to raise than to call. Raising immediately puts pressure on opponents who will often fold right there, unwilling to commit chips to their marginal hands. Or they will see the flop but will be ready to drop out against further bets if it doesn't connect strongly enough with their cards—which happens most of the time.

5. WIN CHIPS, NOT POTS

You want to win chips and to do so, you need to win pots, particularly big ones if you can. So keep this in mind: It is not the quantity of pots you win, but the quality of them that matters. Anyone can win pots. If your goal was to win more pots than your opponents, it is easily achieved by frequent bluffing. However, that kind of strategy will lead to big losses and small wins.

6. FOLD LOSING HANDS

Part of winning is minimizing losses when you have the second best hand. This means not chasing pots when you are a big underdog to win, especially longshot draws against heavy betting. You can't win them all. Save your chips for better opportunities. Cutting losses on hands you lose adds to overall profits.

7. PATIENCE

Hold'em is a game of patience. You will often go long stretches between good hands. Winning players exercise patience and wait for situations where they can win chips. Your good hands will come, and if you haven't blown yourself out trying to force plays, you'll be able to take advantage of them and win some nice pots for yourself.

2. LIMIT HOLD'EM STRATEGY

In limit hold'em, where all betting is in a two-tier structure, such as $3/$6 or $5/$10, the three main factors to consider when deciding how to play a hand are the strength of your starting cards, where you are sitting relative to the button, and the action that precedes your play. There are other considerations that enter into the mix, such as the cost of entering the pot and the aggressiveness or tightness of the table, but you should always consider these three fundamental factors first.

STARTING CARDS

The biggest mistake novices and habitually losing players make in hold'em is playing too many hands. Each call costs at least one bet. They compound this mistake when they catch a piece of the flop—but not enough of it—leading to more inadvisable bets and raises when they are holding a losing hand, thus making the situation even more costly. These lost chips add up quickly and set the stage for losing sessions.

So the foundation of playing winning hold'em is starting with solid cards, that is, playing the right cards in the right positions.

We'll divide the starting hands into four different categories: Premium, Playable, Marginal, and Junk.

Premium Starting Hands
A-A   K-K   A-K   Q-Q   J-J

Limit hold'em is a game of big cards. Aces, kings, queens, jacks, and A-K are the best starting hands. They are strong enough to raise from any position at the table and should be played aggressively. You hope to accomplish two things with the raise. First, you want to get more money into the pot on a hand in which you're probably leading, and second, you want to protect that hand by narrowing the field of opponents.

The greater the number of players who stay in the pot, the greater the chances that a weaker hand will draw out and beat your premium hand.

If a player raises ahead of you or reraises behind you, reraise with aces and kings, and just call with the other premium hands and see how the flop goes. Jacks are weaker than the other big pairs because there is about a 50 percent chance that an overcard, a queen, king, or ace will come on the flop, making your hand vulnerable.

If an overcard flops when you have jacks, queens, or even kings, or you miss entirely with A-K, you have to think about giving up on these hands if an opponent bets into you or check-raises. For example, if the flop is Q-7-6 and you have A-K or J-J, and an opponent leads into you, you're probably donating chips. A better flop would be K-10-3 for A-K or 10-8-2 for J-J.

It's also tough to play high pairs against an ace flop since players will often play starting cards containing an ace. And in low-limit games, you'll get players seeing the flop with all sorts of hands, so if there are a bunch of players in the pot, you have to be concerned about an ace flopping when you have a big pocket pair, such as kings. If you have A-K, however, that flop puts you in a strong position, especially in a game where opponents like to play ace-anything.

You're also concerned with flops of three connecting cards, such as 8-9-10 and three suited cards if you don't have the ace of the same suit for a powerful **flush draw**—four cards of one suit needing one more card of that suit to complete a flush. These are not good flops for big pairs or an A-K.

Playable Starting Hands
A-Q   A-J   A-10   K-Q   10-10   9-9   8-8

These starting hands should be folded in early position. They should also be folded in middle or late position if the pot has been raised from early position, which suggests strength, unless you think the raiser is loose and you can see the flop for just that one bet.

If players **limp** into the pot before you—that is, if they just call the bet—you can limp in as well with the Playable hands. Sometimes a raise will be good if you can force out players behind you and isolate the limper. However, if you're in there against loose players who are not easily moved off a pot, which will generally be the case in low limit Internet poker games, you might consider calling. When you're up against opponents who cannot be chased by raises, you'd prefer to see the flop for one bet with these hands.

If you enter the pot and it gets raised after you, you have to make a decision. If the raise comes from late position and it's from a loose player, you have more reason to call then to fold. It's just one bet. However, if it's raised twice and costs you two more bets, or it looks like you might be trapped between a bettor and a raiser, get away from these hands while it's still cheap. There is too much strength against you.

What if no one has entered the pot before you? If you're in middle or late position, you should raise coming into the pot and try to limit the field or even better, get the blinds.

Marginal Starting Hands
7-7   5-5   3-3   6-6   4-4   2-2

K-J   Q-J   K-J   Q-10   K-10   J-10

A-X (Ace with any other card)

Suited connectors: 5-6, 6-7, 7-8, 8-9, 9-10

Play marginal hands only if you can get in for one bet—but not at the cost of two bets. This means you'll fold these hands in early and middle position where you are vulnerable to being raised.

In late position, call in an unraised pot, but if the pot has already been raised from early or middle position or you are between a bettor and a potential raiser, these marginal cards become unprofitable and should be folded.

If there is a raise after you enter the pot, you can call with these marginal hands when the cost is only one bet, but fold in the face of a double raise or in situations where yet another raise can follow.

Playing Late Position

You can play many more hands from late position. You've had a chance to see the betting before it reaches your position. If the action is heavy, you fold all non-premium hands. If the action is light and the cost is cheap, you can get more creative. And if no one has entered the pot, you should often raise, as there is a good chance no one will call and you'll get the blinds.

If there are only limpers, you add **suited connectors**— hands that are consecutive in rank (such as 5-6 or 8-9) and in the same suit—to your starting hands. Suited connectors are best played in a pot with three or more players. You want multiple opponents in the pot so that you can win a bunch of chips if you hit your hand. If the pot is raised and it would cost you two bets to play, call only if it looks like there will be enough players in to see the flop.

Pairs of twos through sevens are played similarly to connectors preflop. You want to play them in late position when you can see the flop cheaply and get a multiway pot. If there are several callers, you should call, but if the pot has been raised, meaning it will now cost you two bets to play, you can quietly muck the small pair. If you've already bet and the pot gets raised, you can call that extra bet as long as you feel that you won't get trapped and raised again.

Though a pair will only improve to a three of a kind hand about one time in eight, when it does, you'll be sitting with a big hand that can trap opponents for a lot of chips. If it doesn't improve and there are overcards on the flop, you probably have the worst of it and should fold against an opponent's bet. One rule of thumb here—no set, no bet.

Junk Hands

All other hands not shown in the above three categories should be folded. They are heavy underdogs with little chance of winning. If you're in the big blind and the pot is unraised, by all means take the flop for free. If you're in the small blind and it costs you only half a bet to see the flop, it's often a good play. But if it costs you a full bet to see the flop, fold immediately. It's cheaper watching this round as a bystander.

THE FLOP AND BEYOND

If you miss the flop and think that betting will cause your opponent to fold, make the play. Otherwise, don't throw chips at longshots. Save them for better spots.

Be careful playing flush and straight draws unless they're to the **nuts**—the best hand possible given the cards on board. For example, you don't want to play a straight draw if there is a flush draw on board, or if you have, say the 6-7 on a board of 7-8-9-10-X. Any opponent with a jack will bust you here. And given that many players like to play J-10, that 7-8-9 flop is dangerous to your hand.

3. NO-LIMIT HOLD'EM STRATEGY

In no-limit hold'em, your entire stack of chips is at risk on every single hand—as are those of your opponents. One big mistake and they're gone. In limit hold'em, one bet is only one bet. In no-limit, that one bet could be the defining moment of your game because it could be for all your chips.

And that changes the way you play hands.

THE PREFLOP: EARLY POSITION

The best starting cards in no-limit hold'em are the **premium hands**—pocket aces, kings, queens, jacks, A-K, and A-Q. In an unraised pot, bring these hands in for a **standard raise**—three times the size of the big blind—in early position. So if the big blind is at $5, make your raise $15, and if it's $10, make your raise $30.

Your goal is to narrow the field to one or two callers and either to win the pot right there when all players fold, or to reduce the number of players who will see the flop.

If you have aces or kings, hopefully you'll get a caller or two, or even better, a raiser. Then you'll raise right back the size of the pot or go in for all your chips if you get reraised. With queens and A-K, you can stand a raise to see the flop, but if the raise is for all your chips, you may need to let these hands go.

If you don't want your day finished with queens, you certainly don't want to go out on jacks or A-Q! If an opponent goes all-in when you hold J-J or A-Q, or even puts in a big raise, these are grounds for folding these hands.

If a player comes in raising before you, the aces and kings are automatic reraises and the non-premium hands are automatic folds. Lean towards calling with A-K and queens. If the raiser is tight, fold with A-Q and jacks; if the raiser is loose, raising or calling are both viable options. Remember that no play is set in stone in no-limit hold'em. You need to judge hands on a situation by situation basis.

Pass on all other hands from early position.

MIDDLE POSITION

In middle position, you can play more hands due to the simple fact that you have fewer players behind who can raise your bets. If there is a raise before your turn, consider folding all non-premium hands. You don't want to go into the flop as a big underdog, which an earlier position raise probably indicates. And if the raiser is tight, fold jacks and A-Q as well. If you have aces or kings, reraise and have no fear of getting all your chips in the middle. You can also reraise with queens and A-K, or you could just call.

If no one has raised in front of you, you will still play the premium hands for a raise and can add the second tier hands— eights, nines and tens, along with A-J, A-10, and K-Q to your list of raising hands. If you get reraised by a player behind you, consider throwing second tier hands away. These hands have value but against heavy betting, they're chip burners.

Of course, if your opponent is low on chips and moves in on the preflop, especially in a tournament, give him credit for holding lesser quality cards and be prepared to play all premium hands—but again, use judgment.

LATE POSITION

In late position, if the pot has been raised in early position, reraise with A-A, K-K, Q-Q, and A-K. If you get reraised, you may consider just calling with Q-Q and A-K, and if the raiser is tight and goes all-in, you probably want to release these hands. And you certainly do not want to be in that reraised pot with jacks, A-Q or anything less. With aces and kings, you're always ready to play for all the marbles preflop.

If the pot is raised in middle position, reraise with the top four hands, A-A, K-K, Q-Q, and A-K. How you play jacks and A-Q is a judgment call, but it may be safer to just call and see the flop.

If there has been no raiser in the pot, you can expand your starting hands to any pair, an ace with any other card, and any two cards 10 or higher, for example, Q-10 or K-J. Generally, it's best to come in raising. Most of the time, you'll win the blinds, which is good. If you get callers, you have some value to see the flop.

If you get aces or kings in late position, and you think you'll get a caller, raise. If not, it might be better to limp in. You don't get kings or aces often, and when you do, you want to make money on them.

You can also play suited connectors, such as 6-7, 7-8, 8-9, and 10-J, if you can see the flop cheaply.

THE BLINDS

If everyone folds to you in the small blind or there are only callers and you can see the flop cheaply, it's not a bad play to throw a few chips in there for the call. You may flop something pretty and be able to take down a big pot if you get played with, or you may end up checking to the showdown and winning with better garbage than your opponent.

Same with the big blind. If there is no raise and you're in the big blind, and you're not in a raising situation, always see it for free—don't make the mistake of folding!

If there's a raise from early or middle position, fold anything but premium hands. You're asking for trouble to bump up against players showing strength, especially when you'll have to act before them on the next three betting rounds.

However, if a late position bettor continually raises your big blind, then you have to take a stand at some point to keep him in line. You'd like to have two big cards or ace-anything to reraise with, but you can also do this with garbage. If you read him correctly, he'll fold and you've got *his* chips. Do this once or twice and you'll get his attention and respect.

THE FLOP

When the flop hits the board, the real play in hold'em begins. Unless you have the **nuts**, the absolute best hand possible given the cards on board, nothing is for sure when the flop hits the table. You might flop great, but an opponent might have flopped better. But most of the time, you'll flop nothing, with your opponents in the same predicament.

So who gets the pot when neither player makes a powerful hand?

In no-limit, it is the player who goes out and gets it. Betting, raising, and putting pressure on opponents causes them to fold. The great players keep pushing their opponents with bets and raises and take the pot right there or on the next betting round with continued aggressive play. If that doesn't work, they're able to read their opponents for strong hands and fold before they lose too many chips and get hurt.

If you came in raising preflop, you want to continue playing aggressively. If you're first, make a pot-sized bet about three out of five times, regardless of what flops. (You don't always want to raise here and become predictable.) Your opponent will probably fold and you've got the pot. If he calls and you don't improve, you might consider checking on the turn. If he raises you, it's a tough call, but you'll have to consider giving up the hand unless you feel you've got better. Now, if you're second, and he checks, bet out at him.

What if he bets into you? If you miss the flop, give him the pot. Since you've shown strength preflop, his bet on the flop means you're probably second-best.

When you have what you think is the best hand, your goal is to take the pot immediately, particularly when there are straight and flush draws possible, for example, two cards of the same suit are on the board. You don't want opponents playing for another card cheaply, making it, and then destroying you on a hand that shouldn't have even seen another card. If opponents are going to beat you, make them pay to do so.

However, if you have an absolute monster like a full house or quads, you want to keep players in and extract more bets out of them. Often, that means checking and hoping a free card gives them a bigger hand.

THE TURN

If you've played aggressively on the preflop and flop, and your opponent hasn't budged, you have to figure him for possible strength. It's time for you to look at what you think *he thinks* you have. If you're representing strength and playing tight, you have to give him credit for a strong hand and slow down your betting. If he checks, you check, and if you're first, check to him and see how he reacts.

The more chips you bet, the more encouragement an opponent has to fold, but at the same time, the more risk you take if he doesn't fold and has the better hand. At the same time, overbetting the pot to force an opponent to fold risks more chips than necessary if fewer chips will do the same job.

If you think a bet will get an opponent to lay down stronger cards, make that bet. If you think you've got the best hand, try to get more chips into the pot. You don't want to give opponents a chance to improve for free.

THE RIVER

When you have a big hand that you're confident is the best, you want to get more chips into the pot. If you're last and there have been no bets, put the amount of chips in the pot you feel your opponents will call. If you're first, you have two options: check or bet. If your opponent is very aggressive or has been leading at the pot, you can consider checking and letting him bet, then going over the top of him with a raise to try and get even more chips in the pot. You want to be careful not to move an opponent off a pot when you have the best hand. Let your knowledge of how your opponent plays guide you.

If you have doubts whether your hand is the best one out there, and you're first to act, it's often better to check at the river, rather than bet and risk a big raise or an all-in that you will take you out of a pot you may have won. You can also bet a small amount, giving your opponent an opportunity to call (and not get a free ride to the showdown), leaving him room to fold, and not exposing yourself too much if he goes over the top.

If your opponent goes first and checks, you can see the showdown with no further cost. If he bets, you see what you want to do. If there are enough chips in the pot, and his bet isn't going to cripple you, you often get good pot odds to make a call. Before you call a river bet or fold (or raise), think the hand over carefully—with a lot of chips on the line, this is not a time to rush into a decision.

If you're going to bluff at the river, however, make sure it's for enough chips so that your opponent will be faced with a tough decision.

4. SEVEN-CARD STUD STRATEGY

Enter the pot only with cards that have the right winning ingredients. These are the minimum starting cards you should play in seven-card high stud:

- Three of a kind
- Three-card straight flush
- Three-card flush
- Three-card straight
- Pair of tens or higher
- Low or middle pair with ace or king kicker
- Concealed pair with face card kicker
- Three high cards, two of them suited

With **three of a kind**, you are heavily favored to win and want to keep as many players in the pot as possible. Play low key on third and fourth street, calling bets but not raising. With **three-card flushes and straights**, call third street betting, but do not raise. If your draw doesn't improve by fourth street, fold the hand. **Pairs of tens or higher** should be played aggressively to narrow the field, particularly aces, kings and queens if there is no card higher than the kicker showing on the board. Play **low and middle pairs** only if an ace or a king is held as a side card. If you pair up the ace or king, it gives you a good chance to win, unless you have the kings and an opponent shows an ace. **Concealed pairs with a face card kicker** give you hidden strength while **three high cards with two of them suited** are good drawing hands.

You must pay attention to all the open cards in seven-card stud. Open cards held or folded by opponents cannot be drawn by you (or other players) and greatly impact the chances of improving a hand. If you hold a marginal hand and are unsure of how to proceed, lean toward folding if cards you need are already in play and toward playing if they are not. Similarly, pay attention to cards that your opponents need that are no longer in play, as it makes it more difficult for them to improve their hand. For example, if an opponent has a king showing on third street, but two other players have folded kings and you hold one yourself, you know it's impossible that he's paired his kings since there are only four of them in the deck.

5. FIVE-CARD STUD STRATEGY

Of all the forms of high poker, the final winning hands in five-card stud will be the weakest. After all, if played to the river, you'll only see five total cards. Compare that to hold'em and seven-card stud, where seven cards will be used to from the final five-card hand, or even Omaha, where nine cards will be seen.

So, with just five total cards, this makes your starting cards even more critical than in the other poker variations. You need good values to enter the pot. Hands that start weak put you at a disadvantage because they tend to end weak.

More than any other main poker version, five-card stud is a game of high cards *and* live cards. With only five cards to work with, the final high hand may simply be an ace- or king-high hand, or a low pair. Players holding low pairs, though the hand may end up best, have to fear higher pairs. Two pair and three-of-a-kind hands will not often be held, and in the latter case, your opponent would have to have two of his three identical ranks showing on board. Likewise with straights and flushes: For an opponent to hold one of these strong hands, you'd easily know by his upcards whether he even had a chance at one. For example, if an opponent holds 6-8-J of mixed suits on fourth street, you know he can't possibly get a flush or a straight, nor could he hold three of a kind.

With the majority of your cards being open at five-card stud (80 percent of them by the river), five-card stud is the easiest of the poker games to put an opponent on a hand. If you're beaten on board and bets are due you, you'll have to ask yourself, "What am I doing in this pot?" Unless you have a really good answer, say *sayonara*—fold and save your chips.

You want to pay attention to cards that are folded and out of play so you're aware of dead cards, ranks, or suits that can no longer help you or your opponents.

> **INSIDER TIP**
>
> ## BEWARE AGGRESSIVE BETTING FROM LOW UPCARD HANDS
> Suspect players betting strong with low upcards to be either paired or to hold an overcard to the board, likely an ace or perhaps a king.

STARTING HANDS

On the first round of betting, you know half your opponent's current hand. If he has a 6 as his open card, you know the best hand he could hold is a pair of sixes; and his second-best hand would be an A-6. If you hold a pair higher than sixes, you're a favorite over that player no matter what his current hand might be.

As a general rule, you don't want to put any money into the pot unless you hold a pair, or one of your two cards is higher than any card on board—and is *live*, that is, no other player holds that card. For example, if you have a jack on board with a queen in the hole, you're an underdog to any player with a king or ace. And if your opponent's king or ace is showing on board, you're playing at a disadvantage, not only to that big overcard, but to any player also contesting the hand who may be better.

In a nutshell, don't enter the pot unless the hand you hold can beat, or at least tie, the highest card on board.

MINIMUM OPENING REQUIREMENTS

Any Pair: This is a strong start, especially if the pair is high.

Ace in the Hole: If an opponent shows an ace on board, make sure your other card is at least a 9 or higher.

King in the Hole: Play only if no ace is showing, otherwise fold. If another king is on board, you want either a jack or queen to accompany your king.

Do not play any other hands. Even if you have a queen, and it is higher than any other upcard, it is likely that another player has a pair, or an ace or king, and you'll be starting the hand as a significant underdog. Now and then you'll need to mix up your play and enter the pot with other cards; but generally speaking, you want to start with cards that have a good chance of holding up.

FIVE ESSENTIAL STRATEGY CONCEPTS

1. Enter Only with Good Starting Cards

Enter only with a pair, an ace (or an A-9 or better if another ace is on board), or a king if it's higher than any other card on board.

2. Fold When You're Beat on Board

A pair of kings does you no good if an opponent holds aces. Nor does a king-high or queen-high hand help if there is an overcard on board. You're beat, so fold.

3. Bet with an Open Pair

If you get action or a player bets into you, keep a careful eye on your opponent; he likely holds better cards.

4. Be Aware of Live Cards

Watch for aces, kings, and live cards—especially ones you or your opponents need.

5. Don't Play for Flush or Straight Draws

Make an exception only if the pot odds justify it.

6. OMAHA HIGH LOW 8-OR-BETTER STRATEGY

With both a high half and low half to go after, many players stay interested in Omaha high-low pots, especially in low-limit "no fold'em" games, in which players will chase hands right to the river since the last card dealt can so dramatically change the complexion of a hand. Don't get sucked into the rampant betting that often occurs in 8-or-better, not unless your hand is worthy of all the action. Speculation and loose play can lose you a bunch of chips in a hurry in this game.

FOUR KEY CONCEPTS
1. Scooping
In high-low games of any type, there is one guiding principle that is the foundation of all winning strategies: Play hands that have a chance to scoop the pot, that is, win both the high and low half of the pot. This is especially true in Omaha, particularly pot-limit versions.

2. Aces
The best card in Omaha 8-or-better is the ace, and generally speaking, if you don't have one, you're best off not even being involved in the pot. And while there are hands that have good potential without the ace, if you're a beginner, you can get away without playing any of them and still play a pretty solid game.

3. Play Good Starting Hands
An ace, a 2, or a 3 and one more unpaired card 5 or below is a strong starting low. The best starters in Omaha 8-or-better

have both high and low possibilities, so along with the ace plus 2 or 3 and third low card, you'd like another ace (A-A-3-5), or two suited cards, preferably led by the ace, so that you have a shot at a nut flush. A king is a good card to accompany the ace, for example A-2-5-K, because it's the top kicker to an ace hand with nut-high and nut-low straight possibilities.

Four low cards, like A-2-3-4, A-2-3-5, and A-2-4-5, with two suited cards, give you a decent chance of going low and wheeling (making a perfect low, a wheel—A-2-3-4-5) or flushing to a strong high hand.

When competing for the high end of the pot, hands with A-K and A-A have more strength against fewer players and less value against more players, since straights, flushes, and full houses are more common as more bettors stay to the end. You can start with some high-only hands, but if you do, all four of the cards must be **coordinated**, that is, close in rank to one another. Thus, a hand like K-K-Q-J would be good, but K-K-Q-7 would not. That 7 is a **dangler**, meaning that it doesn't coordinate with the other cards.

4. Playing for the Nuts

With so many players seeing the flop and playing through to the river, it is important that you start out with hands that have the potential to be the nuts, the best hand possible given the cards on board. In other words, if you can make a flush, it should be the best flush (one led by an ace), and if it's a straight, then you don't want the ignorant, or low end of the straight. When you're going for low, your hand should have the potential to be the best possible low.

THE FLOP AND BEYOND

The more players remaining to see the flop, the better your hand must be. In particular, you either need to have the nuts or a draw to the nuts, because with the loose action common in many games, especially low-limit ones, that's what it's going to take to win.

When making your decision on how to play a high hand, you must consider that the pot is only worth half of what you might normally win, especially if a low possibility is on board. The dilution of the pot is something that regular high or low players often overlook, but it affects betting and playing strategy. That is why hands with the strength to go both ways are so valuable in high-low games.

7. MULTI-TABLE TOURNAMENT STRATEGY

KEY NO-LIMIT HOLD'EM TOURNAMENT CONCEPTS

In a tournament, your strategy boils down to one thing: Survival. Your goal is to hang in there and move up the ladder as players get eliminated so that you can get into the prize money. And finally, you want to get to the final table or be the champion.

In a no-limit hold'em tournament, chips are power. If you have a lot of them, take advantage of your superior chip count by bullying short stacks and timid players with aggressive betting and by stealing their blinds. Anytime you bet and compete against a smaller stack, he knows that if he goes to war with you for all his chips and loses, he's eliminated. It is difficult for short stacks to play back at you because you can break them. Conversely, when you're that smaller stack, you must tread carefully against bigger stacks because your tournament will be at stake if all the chips go in the middle.

If you get **low-stacked**—that is, your chip stack is less than five times the size of the big blind—then you need to make a play for all your chips at the very first opportunity. If the pot is unraised and you have an ace with any other card, two cards 10 or higher, or any pair, go all-in and hope for the best. You cannot afford to play passive here—calling is not an option—you need the blinds and antes to stay alive.

Ideally, you would like your stack size to be at least ten times the size of the big blind. Either you take risks or you will get **blinded out**—lose all or a majority of your chips to the gradual forced blind and ante bets by barely playing any hands!

The most fundamental no-limit play to get chips is called **stealing the blinds**. This is when you raise in late position when no one else has entered the pot so that opponents will fold and you can win the blinds without a fight. The best position to do this from is the button or the seat before the button. Often, the blinds will fold, giving you the pot uncontested. You don't want to make this play every time, because your opponents will catch on, but at the same time, if the blinds are going to give you the pot without a fight, well then, take it every time.

In all situations, if an opponent is short-stacked, give him credit for much less of a hand than you would normally expect and don't be afraid to play all premium hands for all of your opponent's chips. You can also consider playing back at him with any pair or two high cards if you have a lot of chips and a loss here won't make you low-stacked. Just as you would play all sorts of hands when your stack is desperately low, so would your opponent, so you can open up here and call an all-in bet with less of a hand.

EARLY ROUND TOURNAMENT STRATEGY

In the first few rounds of a tournament, the blinds are generally small, and the antes won't kick in until the third or fourth level. During these early rounds, there is little pressure on you to make any moves as the blinds won't make too much of a dent in your stack, at least not a critical dent. Your strategy here is to play conservatively, trying to win little pots when possible and avoiding big pots unless you think you have the winner. You don't want to risk your tournament on a foolish bluff.

Your goal is to increase your chip stack as the tournament progresses, hopefully to double up after three rounds.

MIDDLE ROUND TOURNAMENT STRATEGY

The middle rounds of a tournament, around levels four to eight, is when players start getting eliminated at a more rapid pace. The blinds and antes are more expensive and this means you have to play more hands and take more chances if your stack has been eroded.

If you're low-stacked, aggressive play and stealing blinds become more important to keep up with the costs of feeding blinds and antes into the pot. If you're big-stacked, you want to push around the weak players and small stacks and get more chips. You're looking to position yourself for the final table.

LATE ROUND TOURNAMENT STRATEGY

If you've lasted into the later rounds, you've either made it into the money or are getting real close. Now you look forward, hoping to get to the final table and the bigger money. You want to pick up your game here and play your best poker. Avoid facing off in big pots or all-ins against stacks that can take you out—unless you've got the goods. As always in a tournament, keep pushing your weight around against players that can be bullied.

FINAL TABLE

If you get to the final table, you have a real shot at winning, but you still have to get through the last players. If you're among the big stacks, avoid going to war against another big stack that can bust you or make you one of the small stacks. Use your big stack to put pressure on smaller stacks struggling to stay alive.

If you're low-stacked, the blinds and antes are exerting tremendous pressure, leaving you with little choice but to find your best opportunity and then go after it for all your chips. Calling is not an option here.

Think before you make your moves, keeping in mind that every player eliminated means a big jump in prize money.

8. SIT-AND-GO STRATEGY

KEY SIT-AND-GO CONCEPTS

Sit-and-go tournaments are typically ten-player tournaments online, though some sites have sit-and-gos set up for six or nine players. The ten-player tournaments are preferable because, after all, it is more fun to chase a bigger prize pool for roughly the same amount of effort.

Like regular tournaments, the blinds in sit-and-gos increase after a set amount of time, and continue to increase at short levels so the pressure stays on players to get in there and mix it up. As a result of the rapid blind increases (and antes that kick in), players get eliminated quickly. And each time one player goes, you get one spot closer to the prize money of the top three places.

With the high blind structure compared to the number of chips you have in play, these tournaments go fast and allow you little room to make mistakes. You'll only be sitting with your opponents for a short amount of time, so your best bet is to play straightforward poker. You can't afford to miss any opportunity to win chips—or lose chips—by being cute. This means avoiding unnecessary bluffs and overly loose play. You don't have enough chips to mess around.

In the first three levels, stick with your premium hands for entering pots. And don't risk too many chips trying to steal just a few in return. You don't have the bankroll for this kind of error. If you have $1,000 in chips and piss away $250 on a steal or resteal, that leaves you with only $750 and a far smaller margin for error. And if you get a chance to double up, you can only get to $1,500 as opposed to $2,000 if you had the $1,000 to start with.

Your goal is to pounce aggressively if you get a good

situation, otherwise you should exercise patience. Some players will drop out of play during these levels, and if that's the case, you've moved that much closer to the money. With fewer players at the table, the value of hands rises and you should play more aggressively.

Levels 4 through 6 call for more aggression, but still a cautionary approach. It is worth taking some risks to steal blind and antes. Somewhere during these levels, as players get eliminated, you'll likely get close to six players and short-handed poker. This means it's time to get more aggressive preflop. There are fewer players acting after you. Also, the blinds have gone up and there are more chips to steal (or lose by attrition if hands are not played!). If you see players who won't defend their blinds, go get those chips.

When you get down to about four players, sit-and-gos (SNG's) become a bit of a crapshoot. Often, because the blinds are high compared to your chip stack, the only viable strategy at that point is making all-in bets. However, the skill is getting yourself in position to get to the final four players.

If you've managed to build up chips and are the big stack or are second or third in chips, you have room to make some plays and put pressure on the struggling stacks by stealing blinds and making pressure calls, bets and raises against them when they enter pots. And if you get short-stacked, make sure to get the right situation to move-in with all of your chips so that your bet has leverage. You hope to either move another player off a pot—especially a timid or small-stacked one—or if you get called, to give yourself an opportunity to double up and get more chips than if you had started with a smaller stack.

SECTION V
25 Online Poker Strategies

1. INTRODUCTION

Players tend to play with a bit more abandon online than they would in live games, with bluffing and aggressive play being more prevalent in cyberspace. Loose players play looser, aggressive players play more aggressively, and overall, more players enter more pots and stay there longer. Much of this has to do with the fact that players are farther removed from the actual money being wagered online than even in a casino, where chips are used for money. Online, you still have chips, but you can't touch them or play with your pile. They become theoretical objects—sort of.

And that makes a difference.

Well, we all know those online chips are not really theoretical—they represent actual amounts of money and thus are very real—but the inability to physically touch them and hold them separates players from the reality of what those chips mean. What they really stand for. It's a fact of life (and poker) that the farther you remove someone from the reality of a situation, the less they can conceptualize that reality. Chips, in a casino, are just chips. They're not money. And thus, they're easier for players to lose than holding the real thing in their hand. And online, chips are not even the game pieces (chips) they sometimes represent in live play. They become numbers. Theoretical—as in, *not real*—numbers.

This removal-from-reality separation has real effects online. There is no shame in losing on a bad play, just the consequences of the bad play—only chips are lost. If a player loses a big bet or a bluff, there is no embarrasment like there might be in a game with players looking at each other face-to-face. The barrier of physically pushing chips into the middle in a live game is removed. An aggressive play can be made with just the click of a button. Click: it's done. It's *easy* to make bold moves; nothing to it. Just click the mouse.

But as I said earlier, whether online or live, poker is poker. The strategies for beating the various poker variations online are essentially the same as you would use for playing regular poker against live competitors. The concepts of playing solid hands, betting aggressively when you're in a pot, and occasionally slow-playing big hands, along with many other ideas, are all valid. And over time, you will be rewarded with profits for playing better than your opponents, and punished with losses for weaker play.

But while the fundamentals of the game are the same, online, you can't look your opponents in the eyes like you could when they sit right in front of you. Thus, all the little tells from a live game that you can use to gather information about your opponents—where they're looking, what they're doing with their hands, and how forcefully they push their chips into the pot, etc.—are not available to you online.

On the other hand, there are tells and strategies specific to online play that are not present in live play, and knowledge of these can give you an advantage over less-knowledgeable players. We're going to look at those strategies now.

2. TWENTY-FIVE ONLINE TELLS & STRATEGIES

1. PLAY AGAINST PLAYERS YOU CAN BEAT

Let me remind you of the most important rule for any poker game *anywhere* if you are to be a profitable player: If you want to win at poker, you have to compete against players you can beat. This principle applies to online and live play, and should form the backbone of everything you think about and do at poker.

Forget about any other strategy—and I'll give you a bunch in this section—if you're playing over your head, you're doomed to lose. You may be a big fish that can bully in a small pond, but if you swim over to the next pond and the fish are bigger, you're no longer the big fish. An amateur boxer may be the big hombre in his gym, but if he steps out into the ring with the rated pros, he's going to get knocked silly, that is, before he goes to rest on the canvas. You've got to compete where you *can* compete.

If you're playing against players who are superior to you, your chances of winning are greatly diminished. In fact, you're a big underdog. It's like the old adage. A player says he's the eighth best player in the world, but is a loser in his game. The listener asks how that can be. The top player replies, "Unfortunately, I play in the game with the top seven."

To sum up, if you're competing against superior players, they're going to have you outclassed and you'll be an underdog in the game with expectations of losing. But if you're the best player at the table, or one of the best, the opposite will be true: *You'll* have the expectation of winning. And that's the situation you want to be in.

> **RESPECT THE FOOD CHAIN**
>
> The key is to winning is to find and play against weaker players, otherwise known as "fish" or "donkeys" in poker jargon. In other words, you need to respect the food chain: swim with the fish and not with the sharks.

Adjustment 1: If you aspire to higher levels, fine; but first establish your success at the lower ones. Climb slowly. The higher the stakes, generally speaking, the better the players. If you find you can't make money at higher levels, then drop down to where you can be successful. Play where you can win, and guess what? You will win.

Adjustment 2: As a corollary to the above principal—playing against competition you can beat—find a table at the right stakes (for your skill level *and* your bankroll) and play there. If things go great at the table you've chosen, perfect. Keep playing and keep making money.

2. CHOOSE AN OPTIMAL TABLE

The great thing about online poker is your ability to choose your ideal table. Live poker generally affords you almost no choice of opponents. The local cardroom, if there is even one nearby, might have only one table available for a game you like. Or, if you're in a big room with many tables but a waiting list, you'll get placed at the very first seat available. In either case, you'll have little choice as to the table you'll play at, and there may be a wait, perhaps even a substantial one.

Online is a different world. There are plenty of tables to choose from and that's good news for you—and your bankroll. (This is why you want to choose an online site that has liquidity.)

If you find the competition too stiff or the types of players are not ideal to your style—perhaps they're too tight or there are too many maniacs—you can easily change tables. That's the beauty of online poker. You choose to play where you want and can keep choosing. Every time you don't like a table, for whatever reason, you can easily switch to another. These are ideal conditions for a player who wants to win money.

From the lobby of the online site you can peruse the various tables to see which one fits your ideal situation before joining a game. The lobby of your online site will provide you with great information about the games being played.

So what do you look for in choosing the table that best suits your preferences? In the lobby, where you choose from the list of games available, the site will display three pieces of important information about each game in progress—average pot size, percentage of players that see the flop, and number of small stacks at the table. Let's look at each one in turn.

Adjustment 1: Average Pot Size. The bigger the average pot size, the looser the players or the greater the number of bluffers throwing their chips around. In either case, there is more money for you to go after with solid play. Here's another way to look at it: The larger the pot size, the juicier the fruit. You have more to win in games where players are pushing chips into the pot.

Online poker gives you a great advantage over live poker in this regard because this information is at your fingertips. In other words, you know in *advance* how profitable the table might be. What an advantage to know this up front! Compare a game with a big average pot size with one that shows slim pickings. The first indicates players willing to gamble, the second, tight players who are holding onto their chips.

Adjustment 2: Percentage of Players That See the Flop. The more players who see the flop, the looser the table, and the more easy money you can chase. When you find that over 35 percent of the players are seeing the flop, you've got a game with passive and weak players seeing way too many flops. That's good. There's dead money being contributed to the middle and you want to get your share of it. If 40 percent or even 45 percent or higher is the flop percentage for the table, you've got a really loose game with lots of chips waiting to be picked up.

Adjustment 3: Number of Small Stacks. If a table is filled with small-stack players (most likely tight and passive, or reckless), you've got opportunities to go after those stacks with aggressive play. Top players make it a point to have large stacks, so if they get a good hand they can extract every piece of value out of it from their opponents. Doyle Brunson once told me that he wants to have the largest stack at his table for that very reason. If he hits a big hand, he doesn't want to lose one dollar of value because he didn't have enough chips on the table to extract maximum value.

But there is a secondary reason to have a large stack. Top players use aggression and intimidation as their two big weapons. More chips, especially in no-limit or pot-limit games where going against a player with more chips can wipe a small stack out, gives a psychological advantage to the bigger stack.

INSIDER TIP

A WORD ABOUT RECENT TABLE HISTORY
Keep in mind that players enter and leave games rapidly online, so the texture of a game can quickly change as players shuffle in and out. Also, while the statistics shown in the lobby reflect a relatively small sample of previously played hands and may be an anomaly to the actual play at the table, it is more likely that the recent table histories will be reasonably representative of play.

3. THE TIME TELL: EARLY ACTION OR PRE-SELECT BUTTONS

A unique feature of online poker is the ability of a player to make a playing decision in advance, before play reaches his position, by using the **early-action buttons**. While these buttons make the game easier to play, there is a downside as well—the frequent use of them can provide information about a player's hand.

Outside of a player's betting pattern—and that is always one of your key pieces of information in any form of poker—the biggest online tell to the possible strength of an opponent's hand is the amount of time is takes for him to react once his turn comes up for play. A player's betting response can come as quickly as instantaneous to as long as the twenty to thirty seconds you're given online to make your play.

Players typically make their decisions quickly in poker. But when a pre-select bet option is used online, that decision will appear *instantly*, as opposed to quickly. That let's you know he's used a pre-select button. The key factor here is that the player decided in *advance* what his play was going to be without even considering how the betting might go. And that can give you some clues on how he feels about his cards.

So, with garbage, a player may select the Check/Fold button, which will fold his hand if there is a bet, or check it if there is not. With a hand that has some strength, he may choose the Call Any, Raise, or Raise Any buttons. When you see a player frequently use the early action buttons, it may indicate that he's a weak player, new to online poker. Or he could be a seasoned player checking these boxes because he is playing multiple tables and needs to quickly toggle between his various games. Or the player may just be an average Joe making life easy by pre-selecting an action he knows he's going to be making anyway.

However, in any of the scenarios where a *bet* is made instantaneously, the act of committing money to a hand before it's a player's turn to act suggests strength.

There are also situations where your opponent takes an uncharacteristically long time before responding. This delay, of course, can be a number of things—he's distracted by something at home, is playing multiple screens, or there is a possible Internet delay—but what it might also mean is that he's got a good hand and is thinking how best to play his cards. Or he'd like you to believe this is the case.

The following strategy tips will help you in formulating your online poker decisions. Keep in mind that, like live poker, no tells are 100 percent accurate. You have to make your betting choices based on all the information at your disposal. You also have to be aware that on occasion some players will use reverse tells. But in general, you'll find early action tells to be useful and potentially profitable.

A. Instant Check

Suspect your opponent for a weak hand. He likely chose the Check/Fold button, but since he was given a free card, he's still in the hand for another card.

Adjustment: Bet into him on the next card; this will usually give you the pot.

B. Instant Check and then Check-Raise

Your opponent perhaps induced a call with his instant check and now pops you back. What should you suspect? Strength.

Adjustment: It's time to reconsider the situation. It smells like a trap. It may or may not be, but you've got to give strong consideration to the possibility.

C. Instant Call

Your opponent likely used the Call Any option, which suggests his hand is worth playing regardless of how the betting went down. He is possibly on a draw.

Adjustment: Rethink the betting; how he came into the pot, from what position, and the dynamics of the hand. See if this helps you understand what this instant call means.

D. Instant Raise

Suspect your opponent for big cards. He is either strong or decided that he was going to bluff at the pot regardless of the action that preceded him.

Adjustment: An aggressive pre-select raise is a warning sign that you should tread carefully. Of course, consider this information; don't use it as your only source.

E. Pause and Check

Suspect that your opponent's hand is weak. He is acting like he has a decision to make, when in reality, he may want to induce a check so he can get a free card. Or, he simply may be preoccupied at home.

Adjustment: Put out a bet and see if he goes away.

F. Pause and Bet or Raise

This usually suggests strength.

Adjustment: He may really be thinking about his hand, which means you should be thinking more about it too. Give stronger consideration to folding marginal hands.

G. Instant Turn and River Bets

Suspect your opponent for strength.

Adjustment: Give more weight to the possibility that this player holds strength and factor that in your decision-making.

4. OPPONENT STOPS USING THE EARLY ACTION BUTTON

The early action buttons most commonly used are Fold, Check/Fold, Raise, and Raise Any. It will be clear when an opponent constantly uses the early action buttons. It will also be clear when he breaks that pattern and gives more consideration to a hand. That could be useful information, but at the same time, it could also be indicative that the player was busy doing something else—on the phone, checking email, or in another game. But do pay attention to the timing of an opponent's bet for online tells that you can use to your advantage.

And pay attention to your own tendencies as well. You're not the only one watching!

Adjustment: When an opponent stops using early action buttons and gives more thought to a hand, it's often because he's giving more thought about how to play a *strong* hand. When in doubt, fold marginal hands in this situation.

5. REVERSE TELLS & MISLEADING OPPONENTS

You can lead your astute opponents astray if you are a frequent user of the pre-select betting options. For example, if you're setting a trap, you can use the pre-select to choose an instant check or call, showing weakness. On the other hand, you can spend a bit of time thinking on a draw before checking or betting, leading savvy opponents to believe you may be sitting with a stronger hand than you hold and to play passively against you for that betting round.

Of course, you don't want to be too predictable with these plays either. Winning poker is about deception and keeping your play unpredictable. But a few moves here and there can win you some nice pots. (And remember that weaker players may not be aware of these pre-select betting tells so keep that in mind.) Note that reverse tells can work the other way around as well, so be aware of opponents using these tricks. As always, combine all your information together before making your final decision.

Adjustment: No tell is an island. Always evaluate your decisions with all your information at hand, because the possibility of a reverse tell is always there.

6. MULTIPLE TABLE PLAY

Once you get comfortable online, you may find it profitable to play two games at the same time. This will allow you to get involved in more hands and theoretically, if you're a good player, more profits. Some professional online players and action junkies will play as many as eight (or more) games simultaneously. (There are players that can play more than twenty!) These players are looking to maximize the number of hands they receive per hour.

However, I would caution you about trying to play too many tables. Theoretically, the-more-tables-the-more-profit idea sounds good. But practically, it's not so easy. And there is a price to pay. Each table you add to your mix adds more stress, more chances to get confused, and will take a heavier toll on your overall concentration. The mental stress will cause fatigue to set in more rapidly and erode your sharpness. At some point you'll reach a critical mass, at which time that one extra table transforms all your tables into a puddle of chaos.

You'll have to find the comfort zone that works for you. For many players, one table is all they can or want to handle. For others, it may be two, and even others, as mentioned above, eight tables. But whatever the number of tables you play, don't overdo yourself to the point where you lose all enjoyment of the game, and run yourself at maximum stress levels. The extra dollars you might make are not worth it, and when you weigh it all out, you'll find that you'll be making fewer dollars—*and* you'll end up playing more hours to earn those dollars.

Adjustment 1: Online poker pros make a fortune playing multiple tables. Not only do they earn profit from beating up on one table, they multiply those profits by taking advantage of the ability to play many tables. There is a lot of money to be made online by playing multiple tables.

Adjustment 2: If you are considering playing multiple games, keep in mind this key tip: Avoid playing tricky marginal hands that show little long-term profit! The concentration you need to finesse victories with marginal hands will be difficult when you're flying back and forth between multiple games. Profits in the other games will suffer as your concentration is focused on the tricky marginal hand. Bottom line: The key to winning at multiple tables is to play high-percentage winning hands and avoid marginal ones.

Adjustment 3: When you know your opponents are playing multiple tables, be more aggressive in marginal situations when playing against them. Their split concentration makes it more valuable for them to abandon tricky situations with small profit potential and makes those situations more profitable for you.

7. PLAY AT STAKES YOU CAN AFFORD

If you play at higher stakes than you can afford, even if you're the best player in a game, you're doomed to lose. One small run of bad luck or bad cards, which *will* happen, is enough to devastate your bankroll and put you out of commission. This is a mathematical fact.

The other problem is that the pressure of playing for stakes that put your bankroll in jeopardy will affect your game negatively, lessen your strength as a player, and make you vulnerable to being pushed around. If there is one thing that people sense when playing poker, it is a player vulnerable to bets and raises. If players feel that you're weak, those aggressive moves will start coming at you. The end result is that they'll feed on your weakness, bully you out of pots, and you'll end up in a tailspin.

Adjustment: Play games you can afford to play, both financially and emotionally. Don't put yourself in a situation where one bad loss can hurt your confidence or cripple your bankroll. Too many things can go wrong in that situation—and will go wrong.

8. OBSERVE OPPONENTS' STACK SIZE

Better players usually keep larger table bankrolls, especially in no-limit, because they want to get full value out of their hands and win the maximum number of chips if they get into a good trap situation. Conversely, weaker players often don't have this as a consideration, or actually they do—they want to limit their downside on a big hand—so they keep fewer chips on the table.

Adjustment: Search for tables with a higher percentage of smaller stacks. You'll tend to find weaker players here. Similarly, suspect big stack players for being better players—until they prove otherwise.

9. ATTACK SHORT STACK PLAYERS

Many players, when low on chips (half the minimum stack size or less), tend to go though the complete table bankroll they have on the table before reloading or quitting play. They often get there after a big loss or an accumulation of smaller losses that leaves them frustrated, on tilt, or desperate for either a quick-fix all-in bet or a quick all in to get rid of the rest of their chips. Online, it's very easy to see who these potential candidates are— they're posted right on the screen in front of you.

Adjustment: Low-stacked players tend to play either recklessly, waiting to dump their chips off the first chance they get, or so painfully tight that you can steal their blinds and push them around. The good news: It won't take you long to see which type of short-stacked player they are. If you get into a pot with short-stacked players, give them opportunities to get rid of their chips. When you've got a hand you think is superior, raise more often—the short-stacked players will be more likely to commit chips if they already have an investment in the pot.

10. READING AVATARS

To play winning poker, you have to keep your opponents off balance so your play is not completely predictable. You want to create a field of deception so that your opponents are fooled into making incorrect decisions on their hands when they're playing against you. When you've got a great hand, you want your opponents to think you don't so you can entice more of their chips into the pot. And when your hand is weak, you'd like opponents to fold and not contest the pot. As Mike Caro writes in his classic book, *Caro's Book of Poker Tells*, players act weak when strong, and strong when weak.

One of the methods some players use is to create screen names and avatars that mislead opponents into believing they're a type of player that they really aren't. Some players figure that if they can throw you off for a while, they gain an edge. A screen name like RaiseHappy or AllInMan may actually be a solid player who wants to intimidate you into thinking that your bets will be raised. Of course, he could also be the aggressive player that his screen name suggests; but often, you'll find this reverse psychology being used by wily players.

Similarly, GoldenYearsGrannie may not be the coddling geezer you'd think at first, but an aggressive eighteen-year-old testosterone-charged player who'll pound you on every street. But at the same time, the name might work for him, because the disconnect between the screen name and the player may be difficult for some opponents to easily overcome.

Adjustment: Pay attention to screen names and avatars, but like all other tells, be aware that they could be what they appear to be, or the opposite.

11. PAY ATTENTION TO CHAT SCREENS

Chatty opponents like to talk, and when they do, it's a great way to pick up information about their game. If you observe the chat box on your screen, you can get a sense of which players are new to the game (aggressive play works well against novices), which ones are frustrated at not getting cards (good opportunity to attack players without confidence), and which ones are on tilt (more likely to play weak hands aggressively). You'll get a sense of the players who are distracted by other games or activities and all sorts of information you might use to your advantage.

Adjustment: Some players will chat away while they are in a hand. What happens if that chat slows down while you're involved in a pot with them? It often means that they're thinking about how to get the most chips out of you with their strong hand.

12. PLAYING AGAINST THE NEW TIGHT PLAYER

Online players, by nature, seem to be impatient. They like to get right in on the action as quickly as possible. When you see a new player enter a game who elects to wait for the big blind to reach his seat (as opposed to posting the big blind immediately upon joining the game), it tells you a few things about the player. First, he is conscious of every penny that he puts into the pot. And second, he's likely to be a tight player who patiently waits for hands. Like everything else in poker, nothing is 100 percent. This same player could be loose, or new and wants to watch a few hands before he is in on the action. These are possibilities. But in general, suspect a tight, careful player.

Adjustment: When a new player is in the pot, give him credit early on for strong hands (until he proves otherwise).

13. PLAYING AGAINST THE NEW IMPATIENT PLAYER

The new player to the table who immediately posts the big blind so he can get right in on the action is typically an impatient player, prone to loose play, and weaker moves. He can't wait to get in on the action.

Adjustment: Give this player less credit for hands when he jumps into the pot and expect him to get involved in a lot of hands.

14. GOING AFTER THE EXTRA BIG BLINDS

When a new player enters the game out of turn, he must post a second big blind in addition to the big blind that is posted in its natural position. Now you have two big blinds and a small blind to go after. This is something that does not occur in a live game. If two new players enter a game at the same time, and both come in early you'll have three big blinds plus the small blind sitting to go after. Occasionally, there may be even more big blinds!

Adjustment: You adjust for the additional money in the pot by playing more aggressively. Of course, don't make crazy plays just to go after extra blinds. But be aware that there is more money to go after.

15. GET IN POTS WITH A FREQUENT RELOADER

Some players just can't get enough action. They go all-in, get busted, buy-in, go all-in, and get busted again. Once you've identified a player like this, you know you've got an action player who likes to mix it up often and with any type of hand.

Adjustment 1: Try to get into pots with this player because it doesn't take much to get him to push in or call your all-in. There are lots of chips waiting for you if you catch the right situation. A potential big opportunity awaits.

Adjustment 2: Frequent reloaders play looser and more recklessly. It's almost axiomatic, though worth stating, that they make more bad calls—especially fresh after an all-in loss and rebuy—when the tilt factor kicks in.

16. PREPARE FOR FREQUENT BLUFFING ONLINE

There is something about the anonymity of online poker that causes players to bluff more frequently than they would in live games. Online, without any face-to-face interaction, getting caught bluffing does not have that stigma of embarrassment as it would in a live setting. Another reason is that online money is less "real" than in a live game. It is a truth that every step of distance you take away from real money that is held in the hand, is one more step away from the reality of what that money really means. And really, it's so easy to click the mouse and make a bet—or a bluff.

In any case, expect a lot of bluffing online.

Adjustment: When you know there are more bluffers in the game, you adjust by giving your opponents less credit for good hands. You should be more willing to go after your opponents' bets with raises, and call more often with hands that you might otherwise fold—assuming, of course, you're doing this judiciously. Overall, you want to play a more solid game to take advantage of the loose playing by the bluffers. You should also look for opportunities to trap bluffers or let them do the betting for you when you've got a hand.

17. PLAY STRAIGHTFORWARD POKER

The greater amount of bluffing online, the frequency of players changing tables, and the many distractions players have playing poker at home, means you should play more straightforward poker than normal. Fancy strategic plays and image-making moves, given any or all of the conditions above, are less likely to get noticed or have an effect, especially if players jump around from table to table frequently. All these moves will do is cost you money. Online players tend to play too many hands and see too many showdowns. You can profit from this by playing solid, straightforward poker, extracting maximum value from your good hands, and minimizing losses with your weak and marginal hands.

Mike Caro writes about the Fancy Play Syndrome, a tendency some players have to make tricky plays, which costs them money. Online, it is even more costly. First, the subtleties of a fancy play won't work if opponents aren't sophisticated enough to know what is happening. And second, the typical online player is often distracted or not around long enough to catch the subtleties a fancy play would require if it were to work.

Adjustment: Simple. Play solid, straightforward poker.

18. ONLINE SESSIONS ARE SHORTER: CHANGING GEARS

It's so easy to hop around online that players will change tables frequently, an opportunity that often will not be available or will be minimally available in a live game. Online, this often gives you little time to size up your opponents and take advantage of their weaknesses. At the same time, you don't need to change gears since opponents might only be warming an online seat for thirty to forty-five minutes and will have little time to get familiar with your play—or you with theirs.

Adjustment: Given that the average player will spend between thirty and forty-five minutes at an online table, you won't need to change up your game much to fool a constantly changing cast of opponents. Setting up long-term traps is worthless when few, if any, opponents will be around to see the play. Try to get top dollar on every hand played.

19. GAMES ARE LOOSER

Online players tend to see too many cards. When you play online, especially at the lower limits, you'll go against a lot of calling stations that won't fold so easily. This means you don't want to get too sophisticated with your play.

Adjustment: When making key decisions, give loose opponents less credit for having strong hands, but also be aware that just because they play a lot of hands doesn't mean they can't get good hands either in big pots. With looser play, pots odds for draws go up in value and should be a bigger part of your game.

20. YOUR OPPONENTS ARE DISTRACTED

Live poker games offer few distractions outside of the table. Players are not talking on the phone while a hand is in progress (it is not allowed), nor are they tending to personal business at the table. Their main focus is the game around them. But playing at home is entirely different. There are a host of built-in distractions—phone calls, books and magazines, television, music, conversations or distractions with housemates, family or friends, and much more.

There are also the many distractions on the computer itself—checking and writing email, browsing websites and forums, surfing new sites. And then there is multiple table play, which can further distract an opponent from the hand you happen to be involved in with him.

Adjustment: If you're not overly distracted yourself, you gain more value by playing marginal cards against distracted opponents who will find it difficult to justify playing those same hands. And if you are the distracted player described above, stay away from these hands.

21. LOW LIMIT VERSUS HIGH LIMIT POKER

The main characteristic of low limit poker games is a preponderance of players that pay to see more cards with all types of garbage. With little cost to see additional cards, a lot of players stay in to see the flop, trying for all sorts of long-shot hands. And it doesn't cost much, so why not?

Adjustment: Play solid hands and look for situations where you can make big hands. Drawing hands become much more valuable in no-fold'em games because they enjoy good pot odds with the greater number of bets in the middle. At the same time, big pairs that don't improve have less value, because with more players in to see the flop, there is a greater chance that opponents will make two pairs, sets, straights and flushes.

22. QUALITY OF PLAYERS

You get all types of players online just as you would in a regular ring game in a poker room—loose, tight, conservative, aggressive, smart players, dumb players and maniacs. All types. However, online players tend to play many more hands, see too many showdowns, and make lower quality decisions than at regular cash games, especially at the low limit games. Some of these players, no matter what you bet, cannot be moved off a pot, and others play so recklessly that they splash chips all over the table.

Adjustment: To adjust for the calling stations, loose cannons and maniacs—players who can offer you good profits—you'll need to play a more solid game, pushing good hands hard and realizing that bluffing is not a big weapon against opponents who will play every hand till the end or are likely to call anything. Fold weak hands more than you would against a tight table and play your good ones aggressively. You also give less credit for loose opponents having strong hands.

23. UNNECESSARY RIVER FOLDS

Sometimes a player will fold on the river when he is checked to, even after some earlier-round aggressive betting. Why would he do this? The answer is that he knows he's beaten; he's trying to cover up a bluff and doesn't want to show his cards. In these cases, there is no need to wonder what your opponent is holding; you already know he's bluffing.

Adjustment: You're playing against an opponent who is more likely to play weaker hands strongly and prone to bluffing. You should be more likely to call this player down than a tight player, as long as you have enough value to your hand.

24. BANKROLL TELLS

There are minimum and maximum buy-ins at cash games online and you can use knowledge of how much money players buy-in for as clues to their playing tendencies. Players that opt for the minimum amount of chips tend to be conservative, tight players guarding their bankrolls. These are players you can push around and steal blinds from. On the other hand, players who buy-in for the maximum tend to be top players setting themselves up so that if an all-in situation occurs that greatly favors them, they don't cost themselves money by not having enough chips on the table.

Adjustment: When new players come to the table, give more respect to the ones buying in for the max (but don't back off if you've got cards worth playing!) and assume tighter play from the ones buying in for small amounts. However, observe your opponents carefully to see if these generalizations apply.

25. PLAY AGGRESSIVE POKER

Aggressive betting becomes even more important online, especially in no-limit games where you can control the size of the bet you make, and the pot that will be built. Aggressive poker is winning poker. This cannot be emphasized enough. Betting and raising causes opponents to fold, giving you a "free" pot, or makes them more them cautious playing against you on further betting rounds or hands. All great players share this one trait—aggression.

Adjustment: Winning poker is all about aggression. Every great player will tell you the same thing—play aggressively to have the edge at poker.

INSIDER TIP	**AGGRESSION WISDOM**
	Too many things go right when you play aggressively and too many things go wrong when you don't.

SECTION VI
Extras

1. MONEY MANAGEMENT

Playing poker or other games of skill or chance entails risks, no matter how skillful or lucky you are, or how easy the game may appear. You must exercise sound money management principles and have emotional control to handle the ups and downs in gambling. The temptation to ride a winning streak too hard or to bet wildly during a losing streak is how poker players beat themselves.

Following are five basic principles for keeping yourself in a safe playing zone:

FIVE MONEY MANAGEMENT PRINCIPLES

1. Play at stakes you can afford and which are comfortable for you.

2. Bankroll yourself properly. (See bankroll discussion later.)

3. Set loss limits. Restrict losses to reasonable amounts and you can never get badly hurt in any one poker session.

4. Quit when you're not at your best. If you're exhausted, annoyed, or simply frustrated by bad hands, players, or life, take a break.

5. Never gamble with money you cannot afford to lose, either financially or emotionally. Risking funds you need for rent, food, or other essentials is foolish. The short term possibilities of taking a loss are real, no matter how easy the game may appear.

---

2. BANKROLLING

In poker discussions, you'll often hear talk about the long run; well, online you'll get there quicker. You'll get dealt many more hands online than you would in live play. There is no waiting time for manual dealer shuffling and dealing, collecting bets, splitting pots and the like—all this is done instantly by the software. You may end up seeing twice as many hands per hour online, and thus a much more rapid movement of your chips. And if you're playing multiple tables, there are that many more multiples of hands per hour that you'll get dealt.

As result, if you're a winning player, there will be *less* short-term volatility in your chips. At first thought, you would think that more money on the table means you are at risk for a bigger loss. However, that's not true. There isn't more money on the table; there is more repetition of that money, which smoothes out the highs and lows. As a winning player, that is beneficial. As any player but a maniac who thrives on precipitous runs of wins and losses, less volatile winning and losing sessions is good news.

The above discussion assumes you are a winning player; that is, your long term results will be positive given your level of play and that of the competition. The same goes if you're a player who more or less holds his own against his opponents. However, if you're a player who loses over the long run, you will lose at a greater rate than before. Two times as many hands, means twice the rate of losses. And if the player with a losing expectation plays multiple tables, then the efficiency rate goes against him as well.

TABLE BANKROLL

As a rule of thumb, your table bankroll should be 30 times the maximum or big bet in a limit game. For example, if you're playing $10/$20, you should have $600 at your disposal to withstand the normal fluctuations of the game. This way, if you lose a few pots, you'll have enough funds remaining to continue playing with confidence. Of course, you can always run it a little looser, depending on the type of game, your playing style, and your comfort levels (maybe you'll prefer 40 times the big bet), but this multiple of 30 is the bare minimum you should bring to the table.

Similarly, if you're playing a $2/$4 game, you'd want $120 (or even $100 will do) and for a $5/$10 game, you'd want $300. If the table buy-in seems large to you for that size game, you might consider going down to a smaller limit game.

In no-limit and pot-limit games, you'll want a bigger buy-in because the fluctuation will be much greater. You generally want a big enough bankroll so that you're not at a disadvantage to your opponents. But in no case should you have less than three times the minimum buy-in for the game, with five times that amount giving you more breathing room so that you can weather the rough spots.

Many pros buy-in for the full maximum at pot-limit and no-limit games to get the full advantage of situations where they can win the maximum amount if there is an all-in and they hold the best hand. It also gives them more leverage at the table. If you don't feel quite so confident in your abilities, you may buy-in for less than the max, or better, play at a smaller stakes table putting less at risk.

TOTAL BANKROLL

If you casually play poker once a week as a recreational activity, you don't need to be so concerned about a total poker bankroll, just what you're willing to risk in that one game. You can look at it as an allowance for your Friday night or once-in-a-while game.

However, if you plan on playing poker on a serious, semiprofessional, or professional level, you need to have enough money set aside to sustain the normal fluctuations common to any gambling pursuit. You'll want that total bankroll to be at least 300 times the size of the big bet to be properly financed in limit games. For example, in a $5/$10 game, you'll want a total bankroll of $3,000, and if you're playing $10/$20, you'll need $6,000.

If you're playing pot-limit or no-limit poker, you'll want more like 500 times the size of the big blind to handle the greater volatility of those betting structures.

The bankroll requirements stated in this section will give you enough breathing room to withstand losing streaks and still have enough money to come back and play pressure-free poker.

Remember, no matter how good you are as a player or how weak the level of competition, you can't always win. If you take a tough loss in one session—hey, it happens. Take a breather, catch some fresh air, and come in to the next game with new energy and the feeling of a winner. You should only play when you're feeling fresh and brimming with confidence.

TOURNAMENT BANKROLL

In straight tournaments without rebuys or add-ons, you can only lose your entry fee. Not a penny more. So it is very easy to figure out your bankroll limitations for tournaments.

In tournaments with rebuys and add-ons, you should restrict yourself to two or three extra buy-ins plus the maximum add-ons allowed if you're still in the event when the rebuy period ends. Of course, if the tournament allows unlimited rebuys, you can keep buying every time you lose your stack, but that is not the wisest policy. Put it this way: If two or three rebuys won't get it done, perhaps you should wait for another tournament or another day to try your luck again.

If you plan on entering tournaments on a regular basis, you need to figure out what you can afford. While you can only lose a certain amount in one tournament, you can lose an unlimited amount by playing an unlimited number of tournaments. If they're small entry-fee tournaments, you may not give too much thought to their cost, except of course, if you're on a tight budget. You can look at buy-in costs the same way as other types of entertainment—a ballgame, concert, or movie. But if you plan on regularly playing big events, you need to map out a budget and see if you can afford the costs. Sure, it's nice to dream of hitting it big, but don't let the dreams turn into nightmares. You must manage your money to guide you through the dry spells.

The reality of tournaments—and this is very unlike the cash games—is that long, dry spells are common when the fields are large. It is not uncommon to find many top players being shut out from cashing in *any* of the events played at the World Series of Poker championships—and they'll play over 40 events. You have to look at the big picture before putting your money at risk. Set your limits before you get into action, and strictly follow the guidelines you've planned out *beforehand*.

3. POKER GLOSSARY

ACT: To bet, raise, fold, or check.

ACTIVE PLAYER: Player still in competition for the pot.

ANTE: Mandatory bet placed into the pot by all players before the cards are dealt.

BET: Money wagered and placed into the pot.

BIG BLIND: The larger of two mandatory bets made by the player two seats to the left of the dealer button position.

BLIND: A mandatory bet made on the first round of betting. Also, the player making that bet.

BLUFF: To bet or raise with an inferior hand for the purpose of intimidating opponents into folding their cards and making the bluffer a winner by default.

BOARD: The face-up cards shared by all players. Also *Community Cards*.

BRING-IN: Forced opening bet in seven-card stud, or the amount required to open betting.

BUTTON: The player occupying the dealer position; also the disk used to indicate this position.

BUY-IN: A player's investment of chips in a poker game or the actual amount of cash he uses to purchase chips for play.

CALL: To match an amount equal to a previous bet on a current round of betting.

CAP: Limit to the number of raises allowed in a betting round.

CASH GAME: Poker game played for real money.

CHECK: The act of "not betting" and passing the bet option to the next player while still remaining an active player.

CHECK AND RAISE: A player's raising of a bet after already checking in that round.

COMMUNITY CARDS: The face up cards shared by all players. Also *Board*.

DRAW: The exchange of cards allowed after the first round of betting in draw poker variations.

EARLY ACTION BUTTONS: See *Pre-Select Options*.

8-OR-BETTER: In high-low poker, a requirement that a player must have five unpaired cards of 8 or less to win the low end of the pot.

FACE CARD: Any jack, queen, or king. Also *Picture Card*.

FACE DOWN: A card positioned such that its rank and suit faces the table and cannot be viewed by competing players. Cards dealt this way are also known as *Downcards* or *Closed Cards*.

FACE UP: A card positioned such that its rank and suit faces up and is therefore visible to all players. Cards dealt this way are also known as *Upcards* or *Open Cards*.

FISH: Weak player.

FLOP: In hold'em and Omaha, the first three cards simultaneously dealt face-up for communal use by all active players.

FLUSH: A hand of five cards of the same suit.

FOLD: Get rid of one's cards, thereby becoming inactive in the current hand and ineligible to play for the pot.

FOUR-CARD FLUSH: Four cards to a flush needing one more to fill.

FOUR-CARD STRAIGHT: Four cards to a straight needing one more to fill.

FOUR OF A KIND: A hand containing four cards of identical value, such as K-K-K-K (four kings). Also *Quads*.

FULL HOUSE: A hand consisting of three of a kind and a pair, such as 7-7-7-K-K.

HAND: The cards a player holds; the best five cards a player can present.

HIGH-LOW: Poker variation in which players compete for the best high and low hands, with the winner of each getting half the pot.

HIGH POKER: Poker variations in which the highest hand wins.

HOLE CARD: Card held by a player whose value is hidden from other players.

KICKER: Unmatched side card, usually referring to a pair.

LEVEL: See *Round*.

LIMIT POKER: Betting structure in which the minimum and maximum bet sizes are set at fixed amounts, usually in a two-tiered structure such as $5/$10.

LIQUIDITY: The availability of many players and games in a poker room.

LOW POKER: A form of poker in which the lowest hand wins.

MICRO-LIMIT: Poker played for pennies, such as games with limits of 2¢/4¢.

NO-LIMIT: Betting structure in which the maximum bet allowed is limited only by the amount of money the bettor has on the table.

NUTS: The best hand possible given the cards on board.

ONE PAIR: Hand containing two cards of the same rank, such as Q-Q or 7-7.

OVERCARD: In hold'em and Omaha, a hole card higher in rank than any board card. For example, a jack is an overcard to a flop of 10-6-2.

PICTURE CARD: Any jack, queen, or king. Also *Face Card*.

POCKET CARDS: The face-down cards that are initially dealt to a player.

POSITION: A player's relative position to the player acting first in a poker round.

POT: The sum total of all antes and bets placed in the center of the table by players during a poker hand and collected by the winner or winners of that hand.

POT-LIMIT: Betting structure in which the largest bet can be no more than the current size of the pot.

POT ODDS: A concept which examines the cost of a bet against the money to be made by winning the pot and compares this to a player's chances of winning that pot.

PREFLOP: The first betting round in hold'em, when each player has only his two pocket cards.

PREMIUM HANDS: The top tier of starting cards.

PRE-SELECT OPTIONS: A set of options that allow you to choose a play in *advance* of your turn.

QUADS: Four of a kind.

QUALIFIER: In high-low games, a requirement that a player must have five unpaired cards of 8 or less to win the low end of the pot.

RAISE: A wager that increases a previous bet.

RAKE: The amount of money taken out of the pot by the house as its fee for running the game.

RERAISE: A bet equaling a previous bet and raise, plus an additional bet—a raise of a raise.

RIVER: The last card dealt or its betting round.

ROYAL FLUSH: An A-K-Q-J-10 of the same suit. The highest ranking hand in high poker.

SCOOP: In a high-low game, win both the high and low ends of a pot.

SET: Three of a kind. Also *Trips*.

SHOWDOWN: The final act of a poker game, where remaining players reveal their hands to determine the winner of the pot.

SIDE POT: When one player has bet all his chips and two or more opponents remain, a segregated pot created for and that can only be won by players who still have chips to bet.

SMALL BLIND: The smaller of two mandatory bets made by the player sitting immediately to the left of the dealer button position.

STANDARD RAISE: In no-limit and pot-limit, a raise of three times the size of the big blind.

STRAIGHT: A sequence of five consecutive cards of mixed suits, such as 4-5-6-7-8.

STRAIGHT FLUSH: A sequence of five consecutive cards in the same suit, such as 8-9-10-J-Q of spades.

TABLE STAKES: A rule stating that a player's bet or call of a bet is limited to the amount of money he has on the table in front of him.

TAP OUT: Go broke at the table.

TELL: An inadvertent mannerism or reaction that reveals information about a player's hand.

THREE OF A KIND: Poker hand containing three cards of the same rank, such as 4-4-4. Also *Set, Trips*.

TOURNAMENT: A competition among players who start with an equal number of chips and play until one player holds all the chips. Players compete for prizes, typically cash, and get eliminated when they run out of chips.

TOURNAMENT CHIPS: Chips used only for tournaments that have no cash value.

TRIPS: Three of a kind. Also *Set*.

TURN: The fourth community card on board.

TWO PAIR: Poker hand containing two sets of two cards of the same rank, such as J-J-5-5.

WILD CARDS: Cards designated as "wild" can be given any value, even as a duplicate of a card already held, by the holder of that card.

WPT: World Poker Tour.

WSOP: World Series of Poker.

4. INTERNET POKER ACRONYMS

2-7	Triple draw deuce-to-seven
4Q	The f-bomb (sometimes said in jest, sometimes in anger)
5CS	Five-card stud
7CS	Seven-card stud
A-5	Triple draw ace-to-five
AO	Add on
B&M	Brick and mortar (Land-based poker room)
BB	Big blind or big bet
BBL	Be back later
BI	Bring in
BR	Bankroll
BRB	Be right back
BS	Bull----
BTDT	Been there, done that
CO	Cut off. The seat before the button
DP	Draw poker
ds	Double-suited. Omaha term indicating two starting cards of one suit and two of another
EP	Early position
EP	Early position
EV	Expected value
FH	Full house
G1	Good one!
GB	Good bet
GC	Good cards; also good call
GG	Good game, usually said at the conclusion of a tournament
GH	Good hand
GL	Good luck
GP	Good play

GTG	Got to go. A player who is exiting the game
HE	Hold'em
HEHE	Giggling
ITM	In the money
LHE	Limit hold'em
LMAO	Laughing my ass off
LOL	Laugh out loud
LP	Late position
MP	Middle position
MTT	Multi-table tournament
N1	Nice one!
NB	Nice bet
NC	Nice call
NH	Nice hand
NHSPW	Sarcastic remark standing for, "Nice hand, sir, played well."
NL	No-limit
NLD	Nice laydown
NLHE	No-limit hold'em
NP	No problem; also Nice Play
NS	Nice stack
o	Offsuit (cards of different suits)
O8	Omaha high-low 8-or-better
OMG	Oh My God
OTB	On the buttom
PF	Preflop
PFR	Preflop raise
PL	Pot-limit
PLHE	Pot-limit hold'em
PLO	Pot-limit Omaha high
PLO8	Pot-lmit Omaha high-low 8-or-better
POF	Postflop
RB	Rebuy
ROFL	Rolling on the floor laughing
ROI	Return on investment
s	Suited (cards of the same suit)
SB	Small blind
SNG	Sit-and-go
STR8	Straight
THX	Thanks
TILT	A player who's lost his cool and is playing poorly

TX	Thanks
TXVM	Thank you very much
TY	Thank you
TYVM	Thank you very much
UTG	Under the gun
UW	You wish
VNH	Very nice hand
WD	Well done
WP	Well played
WTF	What the f- - - (heck)?
WTG	Way to go
YW	Your welcome
ZZZZ	Comment that a player is taking a long time to act

EMOTICONS

ALL CAPS	Online expression of screaming, considered rude and offensive
:)	Smiling face
:(	Sad face
:O	Surprise